COCO

the life and loves of

GABRIELLE CHANEL

Coco's quiet good taste, 1937

COCO

the life and loves of
GABRIELLE CHANEL
frances kennett

illustrated by natacha ledwidge

London
Victor Gollancz Ltd
1989

also by frances kennett:

non-fiction

A HISTORY OF PERFUME
A HISTORY OF FASHION
COLLECTING TWENTIETH-CENTURY FASHION
SECRETS OF THE COUTURIERS

fiction

A WOMAN BY DESIGN
LADY JAZZ

acknowledgements

I would like to thank Elfreda Powell for her editorial guidance and picture research and Marie-Hélène About for her invaluable help in tracking down photographs in Paris.

Extracts from Colette's *Prisons et paradis* are published by permission of Librairie Arthème Fayard, and from Bettina Ballard's *In My Fashion* courtesy of Secker & Warburg. Other sources are credited in the text and bibliography.

F.K.
1989

First published in Great Britain 1989
by Victor Gollancz Ltd, 14 Henrietta Street
London WC2E 8QJ

Text © 1989 by Frances Kennett
Illustrations © 1989 by Natacha Ledwidge
Designed by Andrew Kay

Copyright holders of the photographs are
given in the list of illustrations

British Library Cataloguing in Publication Data
Kennett, Frances
Coco: the life and loves of Gabrielle Chanel.
1. Haute couture. Chanel, Gabrielle, 1883–1971
I. Title
746.9'2'0924

ISBN 0-575-04595-7

Photoset by Rowland Phototypesetting Ltd
Bury St Edmunds, Suffolk
Printed and bound in Great Britain by
Butler & Tanner Ltd, Frome, Somerset

contents

list of illustrations

C H I L D H O O D

Once upon a time there was a beautiful dark-haired French girl, born into a family of itinerant market traders in the Cévennes, a mountainous region in the centre of France. A long time ago, before her birth in 1883, the girl's ancestors had been small-time farmers, eking out an existence by picking chestnuts from the trees in season. When the crop failed, the child's grandparents took to the road, and in turn their son, Albert, embarked with his wife Jeanne on the same harsh business.

The little girl was called Gabrielle Chanel, who would in later life become one of the richest women in France.

Her childhood was spent on the road, travelling from fair to fair. She had her two brothers and two sisters for companionship, and an ailing mother, Jeanne

The convent at Aubazine where Gabrielle lived from the age of twelve

Dévolle, who was plagued with an asthmatic condition aggravated by the hardship of her life.

Gabrielle knew very well that her father was a wayward, womanising drunk, whom her mother loved to desperation. Jeanne had followed him from town to town, market square to market square, often accompanied by her children.

In 1895, when Gabrielle was twelve years old, her mother died, and she found herself, her dim-witted elder sister, Julia, and her pretty younger sister Antoinette, sitting in the back of a rough cart, driven by her father. They were heading towards the small town of Aubazine, high in the wooded hillsides where the Corrèze and Coiroux rivers wend their way south.

At Aubazine was an orphanage run by the Sisters of the Congregation of the

Sacred Heart of Mary. There Gabrielle's father, Albert Chanel, handed over his girls, and set off on his adventures, a free man. His daughters never saw him again.

The two brothers, Alphonse and Lucien, were sent to the Hospice at Saumur, to an even harder fate.

Gabrielle was inconsolable. All her past years had been spent with her mother in cheap attic lodgings, or squatting on the cobbles of small town market squares. She was a street urchin, used to freedom, used to money-changing, used to adults' wheeler-dealings, in a lax and easy life. Being left in the orphanage was, for her, worse than prison.

This period of Gabrielle Chanel's childhood is one which aroused in her the greatest bitterness. She could only interpret what happened to her as an abandonment by all the Chanels – all those numerous relatives dotted throughout the region who did nothing to save her or her sisters from the shame, as she saw it, of being treated as orphans, when they still had a father and a family. It never occurred to her that if the Chanels thought about it – which was not likely given a multitude of other pressing problems, like finding food for their own mouths – they probably felt her father had the right to dispense with his daughters as he saw fit. A Catholic orphanage would ensure they grew up 'straight', which travelling in his company would not have guaranteed. Gabrielle never mentioned Aubazine or the orphanage in any of her reminiscences in later life, and went to strenuous lengths, when she had money and influence, to obliterate all trace of her presence on the records held by that institution. Being left, unloved, at the age of twelve, permanently scarred her emotionally.

The austerity of life at Aubazine, its severely ordered routine, oppressed her and caused unending misery for her next six years. To be one among so many nondescript, pathetic children, working at grubby schoolbooks, bent over their prayers, squabbling over paltry plates of food, reduced her spirit appallingly. There were hours of silence, harsh punishments and a rota of unpleasant household chores. But details remained in her memory and were later a source of enrichment, in spite of her bitter feelings. It was Aubazine that gave her a life-long love of order and cleanliness, a disregard for material possessions, a penchant for the stark contrast of black on white, like the nuns' robes, and their veils, held with a wide starched band across their pale foreheads.

If the Chanel girls' fate was a sad one, at least they were being educated, kept clean and moderately fed. The lot of their two younger brothers was infinitely worse. They became 'Hospice children', foundlings whom the local governing body had the right to place where they saw fit. Frequently this led to abuse worthy of a Dickens novel. Young boys in particular would be placed with a farmer's family and treated as cheap labour. Of course everyone was poor and hardworking, but the Hospice boys suffered even more hardship than the common lot. They would be fed less than the children of the household, were often made to sleep with the animals in some barn or outhouse, or sent up on the hillsides with the sheep to sleep out rough in summer months. Schooling was erratic or non-existent. This was the life that Alphonse and Lucien endured until their teens, when their father's sister, Louise Costier (for some reason always referred to as Aunt Julia) finally took pity on their plight and brought them to Moulins, near her home at Varennes-sur-Allier, where they found work as apprentices. Before long the boys were plying their trade as costermongers, street hawkers like their father.

In 1900, when Gabrielle was almost eighteen, she and Julia left Aubazine and were placed in a school in the town of Moulins, run by canonesses. Most of the boarders were girls from good families, while a handful like herself were taken in on charity in order to have a good start in life. Gabrielle continued to feel the humiliation of her plight most keenly. Girls in an enclosed boarding-school atmosphere develop a thousand and one ways of slighting those in their midst who are 'different' and there on sufferance. They had to eat at a separate table, were given poorer quality food, and left to sleep in an unheated dormitory. Their clothes were rougher and less well-made than those of the richer girls, and their laced boots were hand-me-downs. These distinctions were painful to Gabrielle – inculcating in her a rebellious desire to better herself, to put herself above such insults and slights.

But there were compensations. Her grandfather's last child, Adrienne, was sent to the convent school as a paying boarder. A friendship grew up between this 'aunt' and Gabrielle of an enduring nature. Adrienne was a very pretty girl (both she and Gabrielle inherited their similar good looks from Virginie-Angelina, Adrienne's mother, Gabrielle's grandmother), and was always a more lively companion than Gabrielle's less confident elder sister Julia. Adrienne was also on good terms with Louise Costier, Gabrielle's 'Aunt Julia', and was allowed to visit her quite regularly, taking the two girls with her. Unlike Gabrielle, Adrienne had the security of a loving home, for Henri-Adrien and his wife Virginie-Angelina had now settled in Moulins, becoming a little more sedate in their old age. Henri-Adrien travelled the markets less and less in his declining years, but still turned out in Moulins.

Gabrielle resisted any overtures of affection from her relatives, unable to come to terms with her father's abandonment of her at the Aubazine orphanage. In later life she told endless false tales about her past. Her created self, 'Coco', referred to past events in a different perspective, reworking the life of 'Gabrielle', her true self. In these recollections 'Aunt Julia' was transmogrified into two aunts, not of peasant stock but decently middle class, living in comfortable but suffocating propriety, repressing any normal spirit in their niece. 'Coco' Chanel, inventing, would wander into long descriptions of the boredom of her childhood and her lack of stimulation. She even went so far as to embroider the story that her mother had died of consumption by adding that her father had, in sorrow, gone to America, from where he sent back luxurious gifts, such as fabulous dresses – gifts the 'aunts' would not allow her to enjoy. 'Tenant farmers' visited the house; 'maids' kept the heavy furniture well-polished but were unable to lift the gloomy ambience of the place. One of Gabrielle's biographers, Marcel Haedrich, has compared some of these images with narrative details from Gabrielle's favourite romantic novelist, Pierre Decourcelle. It seems she drew on any incident, real or fictional, with which she could fabricate a past of pathos. Even in her teens she was feeding her brain with fantasies that would later emerge in the language of dress. The fairy story of Cinderella and her transformation by a magical change of attire is one of the best-loved stories of any girlhood, and its essential message, that a physical alteration can lead a young girl into new circumstances, a chance of love and admiration, was exactly the kind of dream that Gabrielle nurtured. The fiction of being sent beautiful clothes by a loving if absent father eased the pain of the truth. She loathed the label of 'orphan' when she really had a father – somewhere else.

In spite of her understandable resentment, Gabrielle found certain small pleasures in visiting her real Aunt Julia. Her relative lived at Varennes, nothing more than a small railway halt in the middle of a flat expanse of farmland. Aunt Julia was married to a railway official and ran a neat house with a patch of well-tended garden. She was a decent, country housewife, and passed on all the art and craft of good household management. All this was a cut above the life of the itinerant trader, yet in her bitterness Gabrielle often sneered at such *petit bourgeois* respectability. (Coco, later: 'I'd like to have come from peasants. I always get on well with them . . . .' How much internal pleasure she must have experienced with these lies!)

But Aunt Julia had one very precious gift. She was a wonderful seamstress. All the girls had been well-taught by the nuns, and could already sew finely, but Aunt Julia added the vital elements of originality and creativity. Besides showing the girls all sorts of tricks, how to make over old dresses so that they looked fresh and new, how to wash, mend and iron smartness into their clothes, she introduced them to the delights of millinery. Gabrielle would grudgingly eye all the beautiful trimmings, artificial flowers, laces, ribbons that Aunt Julia fetched from Vichy, about 20 kilometres away, and spread upon the table. Reluctantly she would watch her aunt's busy fingers, and feel herself drawn to an activity that lightened her spirits and whiled away empty hours. Then the girls would sit together while Aunt Julia demonstrated how to turn a favourite faded bonnet into the latest style.

So in spite of a disadvantaged start in life, Gabrielle approached womanhood enriched by many traditional customs. The life of the orphanage gave her discipline, a certain personal austerity that suited her temperament. Days at Varennes gave her a respect for womanly skills, homemaking, all of which was to prove invaluable in her later life.

The town of Moulins was a bustling, prosperous place; a garrison town, full of dashing young men in several cavalry units. But Gabrielle knew nothing of its pleasures, the cafés and bars where the handsome young officers flirted with local beauties.

Gabrielle's girlhood passed by under the long shadows of Catholicism. Once, in later life, 1940, when the Germans were about to invade Paris, Gabrielle met the redoubtable American Edna Woolman Chase, doyenne of *Vogue* magazine, at a dinner party. Edna relates how Chanel admitted her great fear of war and asked her what she did, to calm herself. Edna suggested hope and prayers. 'She looked at me dubiously. "Pray? I don't think I know my prayers." I reached out and touched her hand. She seemed so small and childlike.' (Edna quietly repeated a simple prayer that Americans teach their children.) 'She looked very thoughtful. She asked me to say it over again and repeated it after me. When the bad days came I hope it helped her.'

How sad that after all those years of study and worship with the nuns, Gabrielle retained nothing of their faith – or at least, professed to little. All she took from her childhood experiences was a stern pragmatism, and a knowledge of how to make a hard sale.

Only in one aspect did the religiosity of her upbringing remain fixed in her memory, and that was in the matter of ceremony. The young convent schoolgirls always took part in the slow-moving processions that wound through the narrow streets of Moulins to the cathedral. Surrounded by banners, candles, effigies, the girls sang devotional hymns. Gabrielle thought she was blessed with a pleasant voice and loved to sing. Sunday Mass at Moulins was an old-fashioned, elaborate occasion, and all the townspeople – including the occasional cavalryman – lined the path of any procession. These small glimpses of a wider world tantalised Gabrielle and Adrienne. Soon it would be their turn to finish with schooling once and for all, and explore the tempting world of this prosperous little garrison town.

INDEPENDENCE

Gabrielle did not choose to follow her timid elder sister Julia, who had left the school to take her place beside her grandparents, selling in the markets. She had other plans. She and Adrienne managed to find work as assistants in a small shop in the rue de l'Horloge, specialising in trousseaux and layettes, and on the side did a little dressmaking for the ladies of Moulins.

Naturally the girls progressed rapidly, for the nuns had trained them to work swiftly with neat fine stitchery. From time to time a *grande dame* from one of the country estates nearby would call in to have something simple run up for her locally, rather than bothering to order from her Parisian dressmaker or couturier. Whereas Adrienne and the shop's owners were unctuously flattering to these grand customers, Gabrielle always held herself at a distance. The hostility she had felt towards the Chanel family for allowing her to be institutionalised hardened into a general attitude of indifference, bordering on contempt, for anyone she was supposed to respect.

Once Coco said: 'I've never known just what I wanted to forget. So, to forget whatever it was – probably something that was haunting me – I threw myself into something else.' This habit of work as escape started here, in the little dress shop of Moulins.

A certain driven quality is evident in many of the early photographs of Gabrielle. Frequently she looks a little sad, or manages only a tight smile while her eyes remain unlit. The causes of Gabrielle's phenomenal success were already forming in her at this humble, limited stage of her life. Sad, aloof, hurtfully proud, she dresses with less overt intention to please or seduce, unlike her companion Adrienne, who turned heads. Both the girls were blessed with wonderfully abundant hair, defined eyebrows, and beautiful wide mouths.

In 1903, when Gabrielle was twenty-one years old, she left her job at the little shop and took equally poor lodgings in the rue du Pont Ginguet. It was her first bid for independence: now some of the clients from the shop came to her directly to order dresses and return for fittings. Not long afterwards Adrienne joined her in the enterprise but unlike Gabrielle she kept up her ties with the Chanel family, Aunt Julia and the grandparents. Soon the girls widened their social circle by stepping cautiously into the other side of life in Moulins, far removed from the quiet streets of the convent school and the cathedral precincts. This was Moulins the man's town, with restaurants, cafés, bars, all dedicated to entertaining the cavalry boys. These immaculately uniformed young officers from the best French families inevitably inspired longing in every young girl in the neighbourhood and proper Moulins families had to exercise the greatest vigilance over their daughters. It was inevitable that with the freedom Gabrielle had acquired by moving into her own lodgings, she should soon be discovered by the cavalrymen. Legend has it that they first caught sight of her and Adrienne helping out at a tailor's shop where they sometimes earned extra wages at busy times. The little tableau presented by the two girls, so strangely similar and yet so different in personality, bent over their work, was enticing and a challenge. Soon there was a stream of callers at the rue de l'Horloge dress shop, and Gabrielle and Adrienne took to having tea or coffee with their young gallants at the places that were their stamping ground: A la Tentation, or Le Grand Café: small-town highlights that were daring and exciting to the two inexperienced convent girls.

Gabrielle's natural reserve and remarkable good looks set her apart from those light women who normally kept company with the cavalrymen. No one knows for sure if Gabrielle or Adrienne succumbed to any lovers; they were certainly popular and protected themselves by spreading their favours. It is altogether likely that the cavalrymen enjoyed nothing more than a passionate flirt with these two modest yet lively creatures, and took their physical pleasure in commercial establishments. Moulins had quite a few of those, naturally.

Entering this light-hearted but not entirely innocent milieu changed Gabrielle's ambitions most decisively. Accompanying her smart set to the most popular entertainment hall in Moulins, La Rotonde, she formed the wild ambition to become a *chanteuse*. This, not dressmaking, was the first means of escape that she planned: a way out of small-town, narrow ways.

La Rotonde was a raucous, low-class music hall, a '*café beuglant*', translatable as a 'bawling bar' for that is what happened in them in those days. The officers drank like fish, pelted the poorer singers, drummed their booted feet on the floorboards or galloped through the tables on imaginary steeds when alcohol made them boisterous.

Somehow Gabrielle persuaded the management to give her a job, and one too for Adrienne: her friend had a miserable voice but certainly looked stunning, and could at least pass the hat round while Gabrielle tried out her singing. They were taken on to be '*poseuses*', or showgirls, one of the circle of pretty things who sat behind featured performers on the stage and occasionally, on demand, got up and sang a little ditty between acts. Witnesses say that Gabrielle was pretty, yet had a certain reserve that set her apart from the other showgirls. There was nothing louche about Mlle Chanel.

It was in this setting that she acquired the nickname that stayed with her for the rest of her days. It is an irony that she found her name during a period of her life that she would forever try to conceal. Like an arsonist, drawn to watch his

Moulins, as a garrison town, was full of immaculately dressed officers

own fire, Gabrielle publicised a name that was first bellowed across a tacky small-town stage. Her pathetically limited repertoire included a Parisian hit song, 'Ko Ko Ri Ko'. Before long the cavalrymen would yell the title for their favourite little singer and Gabrielle would oblige. A second song linked her irrevocably with the catchy name: 'Qui qu'a vu Coco dans la Trocadéro?' That settled the matter. The ingénue of La Rotonde became 'Coco' Chanel.

Gabrielle and her aunt Adrienne, dressed in their own creations, at Vichy in 1906

Of course the Chanel family were unaware of this development in Gabrielle's career or of her newly formed intention of having singing lessons to move on, away from the unseemly ambience of a soldier's hang-out to the real Parisian stage. None of the Chanels was exactly overbearing with familial concern. As long as the girls made money and appeared to be fit and well, not many questions were asked. Adrienne was a well-brought-up young lady, who would keep an eye on her more headstrong 'niece'.

A stepping stone towards Gabrielle's ambition was to secure a season's booking at some music hall in Vichy, that elegant spa town where Aunt Julia used to go to buy trimmings for her hats. Gabrielle was helped in this venture by one of her admirers, possibly her first lover, a handsome foot soldier called Etienne Balsan. (Legend has it that she was 'passed down' to Balsan by his superior officer.) His family were upright upper-middle-class people from the town of Châteauroux. Not nobility: they had made their fortune in the textile business. In the nineteenth century the Balsans had exported blue wool serge, in vast quantities, to be made into uniforms for the British police force, and Balsan himself had been educated for a time at an English public school.

Gabrielle would always speak of him, later, as more of a confidant, a soul-mate, than a lover, though in the limited circumstances of these early years, she may have succumbed physically to Balsan as a way of bettering herself, rather than for pleasure. That would account for her taciturnity. Coco recalled saying to him, 'I'm going to kill myself. All through my childhood I wanted to be loved. Every day I thought about how to kill myself. The viaduct, perhaps, they'd be sorry for a while. But I'd be dead!' By some strange understanding, Balsan was the first to see that this despair, this self-dramatising tendency, could be channelled into a ferocious determination. He really wanted to help her to be happy; for that concern he was to remain a good friend for life.

Unfortunately, Balsan thought Gabrielle had a rotten singing voice, but she made up for it by sheer force of personality. He lent her the money to kit herself out (with Adrienne in tow) with up-to-date fashions, so that she and Adrienne could wow the managements in Vichy. Now Gabrielle's big dark eyes, generous mouth, and elegantly long neck, were shown to advantage in her simple, well-made clothes. The girls added hats of their own confection, capitalising on all Aunt Julia's earlier lessons.

Vichy was another scene entirely from Moulins. An old spa town, it did not cater for the barracks but for the established gentry of the area, and for retired distinguished public servants. Ex-army men, foreign diplomats, especially those from French colonies in North Africa added an exoticism to the assembly rooms where the rejuvenating spring water was available for therapeutic treatments.

This was probably the first time that Gabrielle saw black people among the liveried servants, and spotted quite a few fading mistresses, keeping a discreet distance from their ageing lovers who were residing at Vichy with their wives and families.

Entertainment at Vichy was altogether of a different order too. The better theatres hired touring Parisian acts, and there was no call for the kind of raucous entertainment, yelling at showgirls, as at La Rotonde. But Gabrielle with her usual determination pushed herself forward until she got an audition at a little theatre, the Alcazar. The verdict was hard on her: she had no voice but could possibly succeed in getting a booking if she spent money on music lessons and came back with her own glamorous outfit. (This was the custom: performers came kitted out.) She worked hard to prepare her act, learning how to dance, how to project her undeniably hoarse little voice, and spent a fortune on hiring a suitably eye-catching sequinned dress.

The details of her life grow hazy. In later years Coco fabricated much of what happened at this period, partly out of shame but partly because she failed completely to realise her ambition, to become a star of the variety stage. She was certainly alone, for Adrienne had given up believing that the world of entertainment would lead to great things, and had gone back to the cosy pleasures of Moulins. Etienne Balsan probably kept the wolf from Gabrielle's door, although he had several rivals. She had become a sort of mascot for the cavalrymen from Moulins, who all wanted her to do well. They admired her pluck and fell for her charm. But with no singing engagement forthcoming, Gabrielle resorted to a little light dressmaking, and even took a job at the municipal baths, handing out cups of water in the Grand Grille.

At the end of the season, defeated, Gabrielle was forced to return to Moulins too. Adrienne meanwhile had moved one step nearer to the life of a professional mistress by choosing to live with a certain Maud Mazuel, a raffish lady who ran a dubious salon, where cavalrymen could wile away their off-duty time gossiping and joking with their girlfriends or mistresses. Maud Mazuel was a sort of professional matchmaker or chaperone, enabling girls of no background to come a little closer to their goal of ensnaring a well-born officer for a husband. This was exactly Adrienne's aim, for she had the naturally refined good looks that might enable her to make the social leap from no background to upper-class status.

Gabrielle heartily disliked the ambience of Maud's house, those slightly seedy tea parties and pretentious outings to the races on Sundays where the female talent was paraded. Photographs of her at this time reveal the disdain Gabrielle felt for her trivial existence. She dresses simply, without frills and feathers. Her innate pride makes her stand aloof, in a simple suit and hat, avoiding all the fancy pretensions of Maud's more pliable companions.

Coco at breakfast at Royallieu where she lived with Etienne Balsan

ROYALLIEU

Luck, for once, smiled on her. Gabrielle's protector Etienne Balsan came into a fortune on the death of his father, which coincided with his own discharge from the army. At last he could fulfil his ambition and live the rest of his life among horses, as a breeder and rider. He bought a stud farm at Royallieu in the north of France, not far from Paris and in the heart of horse-breeding territory. In keeping with the possibly passionless arrangement he had offered Gabrielle for Vichy, Etienne consented to take her with him to Royallieu. She would be an entertaining companion for his house-parties and, besides, she had a passion for horses. Etienne did not care one jot for formal Parisian society, or for marrying into the upper crust. He had the money to do just what he liked – entertain his own brand of men, all of whom were good riders, good drinkers, and womanisers.

Gabrielle was twenty-five when she left Moulins for Royallieu. Old enough to take the risk of putting her future in a man's hands. It was, after all, an obvious route out of poverty and a nondescript existence for a girl of her low class. She had a strong sense of being special, worthy of a better life. That conviction compelled her to take risks. Balsan was a decent fellow, and had already demonstrated his protective love.

In later years Gabrielle insisted that she and Balsan were never lovers, even at Royallieu. One interviewer, Claude Baillen, got the story that Balsan's previous mistress, Emilienne d'Alençon, was installed at Royallieu, thus explaining why Gabrielle felt safe enough taking up his offer. This was also the view of Balsan's relatives (who published privately a history of their family). But Emilienne's new lover, an English jockey by the name of Alec Carter, was also a frequent guest at Royallieu. It is more likely that Etienne was glad of a fresh young conquest, to fill the place of his former mistress. Gabrielle was amusing, her unspoilt small-town ways entertained him. She also had a great capacity to do nothing, to engender a peaceful air about her – as she once said, 'I know how to be inert.' Perhaps that attracted Balsan.

Gabrielle was always a man's woman. She had the trait of making every man feel uniquely honoured by her attention, and she liked the sporting, freely-mannered style of military men, most particularly horsemen. They were not intellectual, but then neither was she. She had few close women friends, and those she did keep up frequently fell into disgrace for some small misdemeanour. The writer Maurice Sachs said of her: 'She was not conventionally beautiful, but she was irresistible. Her words were not magic, but her mind and her heart were unforgettable.'

Gabrielle liked Royallieu. It was a dignified, small château with long windows and tiled mansard roofs. Once a monastery, it had a coolness and calm dignity that appealed to her. Etienne Balsan spent a great deal of money restoring it to former grandeur but adding many new luxuries, particularly in the services, the kitchens and bathrooms.

Gabrielle did not assume the role of live-in mistress with the aplomb that a Colette heroine might bring to the part. She kept herself to herself, wiling away long hours in her modest bedroom, resolutely avoiding any flaunting of herself as the *irregulière*, or kept woman, of the house, a role Etienne Balsan did not particularly want her to adopt. Theirs was a sexual friendship, based on common interests. Particularly horses.

In a remarkable display of talent and bravery, Gabrielle learnt how to be a first-class rider, earning if not Balsan's love, his admiration of her courage. Coco liked to claim later that if someone were to bring her a branch from the forest of Compiègne around Royallieu, she would recognise the smell at once. 'I didn't know any people, I knew the horses. I thought it so pretty the way they threw their legs out in front of them.'

In the years between 1906 and 1910, Gabrielle Chanel learnt how to be a fitting companion for Balsan as he became known as a considerable steeplechase jockey on the French circuit. Her determination to meet Etienne Balsan on his own ground sprang from her hatred of the role of *irregulière* – watching the antics of Maud Mazuel's entourage had strengthened her distaste for such creatures. Furthermore, she met many females of this type among the house-party guests at Royallieu. It was not a house to which mothers, wives or chaperoned fiancées paid visits.

Some special spark of imagination made Gabrielle feel that she was destined for better things. If she had to play the mistress for a while, she would do so in order to learn about life from men who had money and self-confidence. Some of their free-spiritedness and love of gaiety undoubtedly inspired her to shape a future for herself; in other words, to turn the situation to her own advantage.

The desire for individuality and modesty extended to her wardrobe. Etienne did not treat her lavishly, or send her to Paris to be decked out in Belle Epoque extravagance. He understood Gabrielle well enough to know that flaunting herself as his mistress was not her style at all. She liked to look modest, a protégée rather than a tart. Coco recalled later that her entire wardrobe when she went to Royallieu consisted of an alpaca suit for summer, a Cheviot one for winter and a goatskin jacket. Etienne respected her wish to be independent and dress as she saw fit. So Gabrielle went to the tailor at La Croix-Saint Ouen nearby who made clothes for the local hunting fraternity. She ordered a serviceable and unorthodox outfit of jodhpurs and a neat jacket so that she could ride astride, an unconventional pose for a woman of the time. She often went out with Balsan and his male friends in the crisp air of early morning while the feather-brained female house guests lingered in bed.

Another version of the story about her nickname has it that it was coined from her habits of taking dawn rides, up with the cockerel. Coco herself liked to claim that the nickname was given her by her father, long before.

In a mixed party with the girlfriends of the set, Gabrielle sat side-saddle and wore the simplest beige skirt, plain jacket and plainer hat, distancing herself visibly from the other *irregulières* with thin muslin veils, bow-trimmed millinery and lace jabots. Her reasoning remained the same throughout her life: 'Nothing makes a woman look older than obvious expensiveness, ornateness, complication. I still dress as I always did, like a schoolgirl.' In these strict, unprovocative garments she was soon to be seen with Etienne Balsan at all the major local racetracks, St Cloud, Enghien, Tremblay, Auteuil, Maison Laffitte, Vincennes and Longchamps: still not entitled to enter the proper circles of society, still a little provincial mademoiselle on the fringes.

But she was approaching her destiny. Sometimes Etienne and his gang took a trip to Paris by train and Gabrielle caught glimpses of faubourg society, elegant women stepping into smart shops while their *porte-cochères* stood patiently waiting under doorway awnings. Sometimes she observed the *va et vient* of society in the avenue du Bois, where wonderfully erect horsewomen rode side-saddle, accompanied by admirers, or strolled in the cool shade of trees, carrying lace parasols. All these images coalesced in her, creating a desire to move on, become a somebody in the capital city. Occasionally she visited a theatre, although more often she took part in larking charades at Royallieu. Etienne Balsan's friends enjoyed a laugh, and their girlfriends had to be robust, bold young women to merit their love.

Suddenly a way out presented itself. A distinguished young Englishman came to stay at Royallieu. Arthur, or 'Boy', Capel as he was always known, had been educated at English public schools, Beaumont and Downside, and had a large private fortune, made out of the coal industry, to support his life-style. Tall, dark, handsome, with a flourish of a moustache, he fitted into the life of Royallieu with ease, taking part in horse races, dressing-up games, and flirtatious soirées. Photographs give a hint of the sexual attraction and devil-may-care qualities he possessed. There was one fact about him that made him sympathetic to Gabrielle: a Jewish background that in some circles put him beyond the pale. Gabrielle and Boy shared a feeling of being outside society; it formed a basis for growing affection between them.

For some time Gabrielle had been making hats for herself and occasionally for other women in Etienne's circle, like her predecessor in his favour, Emilienne d'Alençon. Encouraged by her praise, Gabrielle tried to persuade Etienne to set her up in a little millinery shop somewhere in Paris. Boy Capel thought it an excellent plan, but Etienne baulked at too-public an action, something that would be interpreted as a statement of his liaison with his protégée. Financing a business went beyond the bounds of a well-born protector's obligations, in his view. But he admired Gabrielle's pluck – a woman who could leave all her family behind, to travel halfway across France with hardly a penny to her name and turn herself into an outstanding rider was remarkable enough to succeed in business. In a small way, of course. To pacify Gabrielle he let her use his Paris pied-à-terre, 160 boulevard Malesherbes. If Gabrielle guessed it was the setting for many of his high-society seductions, she chose not to care. Such a notorious setting only attracted *tout Paris* to her doors.

Gabrielle not only had Etienne's connections but all of Boy's circle as clientèle. Parisiennes who were curious about Etienne Balsan's set-up at Royallieu came to take a closer look at his mistress. Slowly, Gabrielle found her business expanding. Soon it became necessary to employ a professional hat-maker, Lucienne Rabaté, who supplied the technical know-how that Gabrielle lacked. She was enticed away from the current most successful milliner, Caroline Reboux. Then, as the little hat shop became more popular, Gabrielle summoned her younger sister, Antoinette, all the way from Moulins to act as sales assistant. There was one talent both the Chanel girls had as their birthright: a gift of the gab, a natural selling talent. It later emerged that Gabrielle would nip off to the Galeries Lafayette, buy plain straw hats, decorate them in her new minimal style, and re-sell them at four or five times their original price. It was a ruse her father would have admired.

Once Coco was looking at antiques in a dealer's shop. She gave him the benefit of her experience: 'If you want to get on well with someone you ought to arrange for him to have a little "find" the first time he comes. That's the way to get customers. . . . Everything is a skilled trade!' That was the costermonger's daughter in her, drawing on some valuable memories.

Gabrielle and Lucienne did not remain partners for very long. Lucienne was of the old school, a diligent milliner who had imbibed all the correct Parisian rules where customers were concerned, rules which Gabrielle flouted. For a start, all these young bloods kept turning up and flirting with her – Etienne, Léon de Laborde, Boy (who lived conveniently nearby) and others of the Royallieu set. To Gabrielle, running a hat shop was a lark. She made no distinction between a titled wife and a well-kept mistress, between an established cocotte and a current *cause*

célèbre. Most women admired her nerve – levelling everyone to the same status of customer. Such presumption was amusing, and some of the grand ladies came back for more. Others found her offensive and, after one curious look, went back to milliners who knew their place.

Gabrielle's affections were changing. Etienne Balsan was still her protector, officially, and did not yet realise that Boy Capel had replaced him. Gabrielle moved in with Boy, at an address in the avenue Gabriel. Gabrielle's business had by now become so successful that she badly needed larger premises. It was Boy, not Etienne, who financed the letting of a larger salon at 21 rue Cambon – the street that would for many decades be associated with her name.

Naturally, Etienne suspected that he had lost his little provincial mistress. A certain amount of pride and loss of face made him cool when Gabrielle and Boy returned to Royallieu for weekend parties. Suddenly Gabrielle found herself in a discreet tug of war between these two handsome, assured young men. But being sportsmen, the changeover from Etienne to Boy was finally arranged at Royallieu in a sporting manner. Legend holds that the three of them cracked two bottles of Bollinger after a tactful but significant exchange of words. Coco remembered it this way: 'I was able to open my shop because these two gentlemen were quarrelling over my little self . . . the matter was discussed by all three of us together. You have no idea how amusing it was, that three-sided discussion that

Impromptu charades at Royallieu: Balsan with Coco in 1907

started up afresh every day.' (This was Gabrielle beginning to test her powers – discovering that she could make men fall in love with her, and win some handsome benefits. Calculating? No, pure pragmatism.)

The moral point at issue for Gabrielle was that she had to have a means of support that would, in the end, lead her to independence, the only true security. The idea of passing from one man to another and having only their 'gifts' by way of income was not her style. Boy could put up the money, but she would work hard to pay him back. It was the only way she would operate. However, Etienne remained firmly in her esteem for his friendship, and she always kept a small amethyst ring that he gave her, till the day she died.

Her life was one of promise. Boy was the partner of her dreams, a wayward, brilliant man who had great intellectual powers as well as the spirit of an adventurer. His unusual background, being a Jew at an English Catholic public school, had left him with a restless, insecure nature. He had to prove himself, both as a lover and as an entrepreneur. It did not take long before Gabrielle realised that he was constantly unfaithful to her. She did not care. 'He found time to cheat on me all day long, which left me absolutely unaffected. It was of no importance. I was so certain that he loved only me.' As with Etienne Balsan, Gabrielle discovered that she had some quality that set her apart from other women. What was it? Originality; distinction. Boy was undoubtedly the first man who admired and respected her, liked her ambition, and was big-hearted enough to let her be fully herself, an independent, yet loved, woman. He was extraordinarily sympathetic. Coco would recall that at this time her 'health' was not good and she was subject to fainting fits. 'Boy Capel cured me, with exceptional patience, simply by repeating "Faint if you want to". He took me wherever there were people and said, "I'm here. Nothing can happen to you. Faint while I'm here."'

The faintings were more like blackouts, sometimes lasting half an hour. Coco concluded significantly: 'When I got involved with the house of Chanel, my health came back.'

Was her inadequacy, faced with 'society' so great that she switched herself off in this dramatic way? Boy must have been a sensitive and remarkable man, to give her so much moral support. And in turn, he must have judged her to be a brave and unusual woman, to guide her steps into his own world, and to express his love by helping her conquer her fears.

What Gabrielle was after was a dream shared by many women: to be able to do everything possible, freely, and yet to be able to hold a man. She was ahead of her time in her hopes and expectations. It is easy to see why the world of entertainment appealed to her, originally. In her era, only the great stars like

Réjane, Bernhardt, Duse had status as independent women with passionate love lives, earning that certain respect that is owed to a woman following a career. But these great figures had notoriety; Gabrielle was after admiration. Most women of the time wanted no more than security in marriage; self-fulfilment was a dream hardly ever realised by them.

At heart Gabrielle had a burning, idealistic passion: 'The greatest flattery that one person can offer another is carnal pleasure, and only carnal pleasure, because reason has no share in it and there can be no question of merit, and because it is addressed not to the character of the person but the person himself.' There is a brave honesty about her attitude.

Boy gave her polish to add to her self-confidence by encouraging her to read, introducing her to well-educated friends, even to his own family. Gabrielle became closely attached to his younger sister Bertha. New acquaintances were of great influence, particularly the actress Gabrielle Dorziat and the opera singer Martha Davelli. Her roles at the Opéra Comique included Carmen and Tosca, and she was the first to sing Reynaldo Hahn's *Nausicaa*. She and Gabrielle had a striking resemblance to each other, which confirmed their friendship at once. These theatrical stars liked the insouciant little miss in the rue Cambon, producing her extraordinary bold, big-brimmed hats. Before long, the name 'Chanel' began to appear in fashion magazines like *Les Modes*, and her hats on the heads of these currently popular theatrical stars.

With these new artistic connections, Gabrielle flourished, being freed from her conventional terror of being a *demi-mondaine*. She began to see that other rules were being broken, that the old order of society was changing. She was present at that scandalous occasion in 1913 when the whole of Paris booed and jeered Stravinsky's revolutionary ballet, *Le Sacre du Printemps*. She began to notice that 'advanced' women were wearing loose, exotic robes created by the then leading designer, Paul Poiret. (Born in 1879, the son of a prosperous cloth merchant, Poiret worked for the grand old couture houses of Cheruit, Doucet and Worth, before opening his own salon in 1906. He liberated women from the 'S' bend corsets of the previous era, making loose, floating, tunic dresses, all heavily influenced by eastern ethnic costumes such as kimonos, harem pants, turbans, and floating, fur-trimmed cloaks. Much of his drama and colouring came from the popularity of the work of Léon Bakst for the Ballets Russes, first seen in Paris in 1909. Isadora Duncan was a favourite client.)

Ankles were visible, in smart little boots, the curve of the calf definably disturbing under light muslin garments. Proper Parisian society was shocked at the looseness, which as always in history is symbolically linked with the slackening of moral restraints.

Coco found herself in a discreet tug-of-war between two men: Etienne Balsan and 'Boy' Capel

D E A U V I L L E

That summer, 1913, the exodus to the coastal resorts of Le Touquet, Deauville and Boulogne was more nervously motivated than before. The threat of war was becoming serious, adding to the apprehension that the old order was changing. It was in this end-of-an-era atmosphere that Gabrielle took the next major step towards fame and independence.

With Boy's help, she took the lease on a shop in a smart street of Deauville, the rue Gontaut-Biron, between one of the largest hotels of the seaside town and the Casino. Now she began making clothes as well as millinery. At first she used her assistants, her hat-makers, and simply showed them what she wanted – entirely unusual designs. Her first models were loose woollen jackets, very mannish in cut, worn over wide sailor-collared blouses, and simple straight-cut skirts just skimming the ankle. Selling clothes 'off the peg' was quite novel, but in the casual atmosphere of a seaside town, these loose-fitting garments were practical and amusing. Then there were her hats: wide straw boaters devoid of the usual feathers and frills. In comparison with the complicated tucked and lace-inserted concoctions considered appropriate for the promenade or the terrace of the polo club, these clothes were radical, easy to wear and an instant triumph, without the need for boring fitting sessions.

Gabrielle was demonstrating a talent that never left her. In the words of Edna Woolman Chase: 'Chanel had flair and she was a supersaleswoman, if not a creator in the sense that Poiret was, and she was by no means an artist to equal Vionnet, who was unique, perhaps the only true creator in our time in the art of couture . . . Gabrielle's success was due as much to her personality as to her skill and hard work.'

Gabrielle Chanel, at the ripe age of thirty, had found her own style through Boy. It was a casual, unconventional way of dressing that made a woman look youthful, sexually alluring and confident, without apparent effort. She took to wearing a man's fishing sweater, and tying a scarf round her middle as a belt. She sported a naval-cut blazer, almost cross-dressing in a way that was decidedly alluring. Fancy-dress parties and charades at Royallieu had shown her how attractive a woman could look in borrowed clothing. . . .

This look mirrored exactly how Gabrielle felt at the time: buoyed up by her affair with her remarkable Englishman. The Royallieu years had been her apprenticeship: she was more than capable of amusing and challenging Boy, being charmingly unpredictable in her moods from day to day. Boy liked her gaiety, her nerve, her apparently sound head for business. When Gabrielle did not know how to do something, she had the knack of finding an expert and rapidly absorbing what she needed.

He too was on a meteoric course upward, first conquering summering society with his skill at polo, and second by assiduously attending to his industrial affairs. He knew that when war came, coal was going to be an essential commodity, and that as France's African empire expanded, the market for coal, his coal, would grow with it. His fame spread, his circles of acquaintance became more distinguished and powerful. Being a man who challenged society, he had no compunction about escorting Gabrielle wherever he chose to dine or be entertained. Thus Gabrielle came to have first-hand contacts with the rich and the mighty. From being déclassée and a curiosity, Coco became accepted and treated as a personality in her own right. Recalling the beginnings of her fame she said: 'I lived among English people, who don't pay one compliments, who aren't always telling you you're ravishing and a genius. One doesn't talk about these things. It's a kind of spell cast on my life: the English, whom I like, and the Americans whom I like less, like me. The French don't like me, and there's nothing to be done.'

Everything English set the tone at Deauville. All the polo players spoke English. All the language of the turf was sprinkled with English words and the hour of 'tea' was sacrosanct. Gabrielle began to acquire a reputation. Her familiarity with English manners gave her a certain style in the eyes of the Deauville crowd. Her anglicised, borrowed clothes caught the eye. So did her attractive suitor, Boy.

In Coco's words: 'When I wore those men's jackets and the boater, I had an Englishman for a lover. I didn't look at anyone, and the English threw themselves on me like poverty on the world. You see what good luck can do. I found myself in what's called society: polo, tennis, the races. I thought everyone was looking at the polo players . . . but they were looking at me.'

Sadly for Gabrielle this success spelt the doom of her relationship with Boy Capel. Her work began to occupy her more and more. He too had other serious concerns that removed him from her. His business enterprises expanded, and he had to go back more frequently to England. He knew that with the growing anti-semitism of France and the increasing hostility between France and Germany, he would have to consolidate his position across the Channel. His business, coal, could become a crucial commodity in the event of a war. This was his chance to carve out a place for himself in the British establishment. Another tempting course of action was to try and find himself a well-bred wife; to enter into the right kind of marriage.

Unconsciously or not, Boy began to distance Gabrielle by encouraging her in every step of her career. What a cruelty, to be pushed to even greater independence by the man on whom she wanted to depend, to love wholeheartedly.

(In one of her many contradictory stories, Coco told Claude Baillen that Boy Capel was her first lover, and that she had to have an operation to cut her hymen, because she was so narrow. She also suggested that her womb was too small, that she tried to get pregnant with Boy and failed. This is not likely to be the whole truth. A girl who had been as athletic and vigorous as she would quite probably rupture her hymen naturally, while still a virgin.)

Her Deauville salon became the favourite haunt of the most distinguished French nobility – she no longer mixed with the *demi-monde* but with Rothschilds, countesses, princesses, and baronesses. Mathilde de Rothschild could be heard saying, with delighted condescension, 'I shan't buy a thing without showing her. That child's got more taste than the rest put together.'

'Everyone around me was so tactful,' Coco would recall, amused at her inexperience. 'I thought I was making money – I thought I was rich!' alluding to the vast difference between money made and money inherited. For her, wealth meant freedom. 'Money is pocket money.'

War was declared and *tout Paris* rushed back to the capital. Gabrielle thought of following but, on Boy's advice, sat out those first months of the war on the coast. He was, as ever, accurate in his predictions. With the first German advances, not only Paris but half the countryside of France moved westwards and the once grand hotels of Deauville were reopened as hospitals for the wounded.

Not only Antoinette but Gabrielle's other favourite companion from Moulins, Adrienne, her aunt, was pressed into service. The two girls were a popular sight parading around the town streets in Gabrielle's latest creations, attracting comments wherever they went. Wrap-around long coats, with wide, flat lapels, tunic dresses covered with cloaks of a piratical flair; pared-down accessories, such as big patch pockets instead of dreary dorothy bags, and feather boas.

Ironically the Chanels' greatest commercial success was in making elegant nursing outfits for the stricken wives and mothers of the gentry. Simple straight dresses and neat little hats with white headbands, reminiscent (only to Antoinette and Gabrielle) of the nuns' uniforms at Aubazine.

The tide of the battle turned: reinforcements were flung against the Huns at the battle of the Marne. The seige of Paris was lifted. In due course the best families returned home from the coast to the faubourgs, and with them went Gabrielle. Adrienne returned to Moulins almost at once, where her aged, ailing parents Virginie-Angelina and Henri-Adrien died within a year of each other. Another death in the Chanel family affected Gabrielle more directly. Her elder sister Julia, who had made a poor marriage to a local man in Moulins, died, leaving a young son. André Pallasse was befriended by Gabrielle and Boy, and sent to

Coco and Adrienne outside Coco's first boutique in Deauville

school in England, to Boy's old school, Beaumont. His resemblance to Gabrielle led some people to suspect he was her love-child by Boy, but this was untrue.

Fortunately Antoinette was still at hand to help run the business in Paris. Trade was booming: while many of Gabrielle's erstwhile admirers, the cavalry officers of Moulins, died in the trenches, the women of Paris found new freedom in war relief work and a new economic independence. It became acceptable to go out alone, to be seen in restaurants and hotels (a change brought about in England too and a major boost to the demands of the Suffragettes). Without the restricting eyes of fathers and husbands, and often with first-earned money in their pockets, the one thing Parisiennes insisted upon was the right to buy smart clothes. Gabrielle's salon, in the heart of the city, could not be better placed and her simple, clean-cut clothes were exactly the right attire, unpretentious, chic, and practical for their new, active lives. Coco later would self-aggrandise: 'The war helped me. Catastrophes show what one really is. In 1919 I woke up famous.'

That was Coco speaking, but Gabrielle remained frank about her skills, giving others their due. 'The dressmakers didn't take me seriously, and they were right. I knew nothing about the business. In the beginning I had my milliners making my dresses. I didn't know that specialised workers existed. I learned everything for myself: I had to know because I had to explain things to my milliners. Besides, it isn't all that complicated. Fashion is like architecture; primarily a question of proportions. The most difficult thing to create is a well-proportioned dress for all women, a dress that five different women could wear without anyone's seeing right away that it's the same thing.'

The fact that Gabrielle knew virtually nothing about the running of a couture house did not daunt her. Paris was full of sewing experts, pattern cutters, fitters, salesgirls. It was quite common for a head of workroom to be delegated the job of finding her own staff. All Gabrielle had to do was tell her craftswomen what she wanted – and she had enough ambition to learn the art of giving orders at once.

This was not a unique situation in her métier. Couturiers do not need to know how to sew – they just need to have ideas. When Paul Poiret was called up for military service, and found himself in the supply and tailoring division, a disconcerted officer discovered that the great man did not even know how to sew on a button. With Gabrielle, however, the story was different. She absorbed techniques with a fervent enthusiasm.

Boy Capel's upward rise was continuing apace. He had cultivated a friendship with Clemenceau before the man came to political eminence – another example of his judgement and foresight. In 1915 Boy was appointed to the Franco-English War Coal Commission, again a fitting reward for his industrial prescience. He remained steadfast to Gabrielle in his heart, even if news of his other affairs occasionally spoilt her happiness. In the summer of 1915, he took leave from his duties on the Commission and accompanied by Gabrielle spent a brief interlude at Biarritz.

On the Bay of Biscay, the resort had become the centre for draft-dodgers, profiteers, smugglers across the frontier with Spain. The town was ideally situated for yet another of Gabrielle's great initiations in the world of fashion. Only this time, it was not to be a modest little boutique like the one she ran at Deauville. Boy Capel provided the capital for a substantial set-up, a *maison de couture*, on Parisian lines. Antoinette was summoned and the venture began. She organised two workrooms, one of which was the 'creative workshop' where new designs were devised. The other was the production workroom, where individual orders were made to measure. Each workroom held about thirty people, all the way up the scale from apprentices, *deuxième mains qualifiées, premières mains*, and *premières mains qualifiées*. Each workroom was under the direction of a *première* or of a tailor assisted by a second. Once more luck was on Gabrielle's side, for the wealthy women of Madrid, San Sebastian, Barcelona and Bilbao were delighted to have a symbol of Paris so near, just across the border, and proved to be faithful, extravagant customers. By the end of the year Chanel-Biarritz had sixty employees and full order books, and Gabrielle bought herself a wonderful British Rolls-Royce. She was thirty-two years old: old enough to be determined to capitalise on her hard-won success.

Gabrielle left Antoinette in complete control of the Biarritz operation, and returned to Paris to be nearer Boy. It was 1916, and he was in the thick of war-supply work. Not so involved, however, that he could not notice the change in his mistress. The success of her Biarritz operation had exceeded the wildest dreams of them both. She now had young girls from Biarritz transferred to Paris for their apprenticeships, and another workroom in Paris supplying the *maison de couture* in Biarritz with her latest models. Big money was being made between the two establishments. When Gabrielle, prompted by some instinct for self-preservation, repaid Boy his entire investment, he was not only surprised but seriously reinfected with love. That was the contrary nature of their love affair: if Gabrielle became too dependent on him, he withdrew. But if he thought he was losing her, not to another man but to her burgeoning empire, he wanted her back.

This unresolved state of affairs continued until 1917. In that year Boy Capel published a political work, *Reflections on Victory*, which, among other novel and far-sighted ideas, put forward the notion of a European federation of states. He had grasped, more clearly than many of his contemporaries, that the rehabilitation of Germany would be essential to a lasting European peace. 'Arthur Capel' won a respectful regard for his ideas, and the old image of him as a Francophile playboy was finally obliterated by his *gravitas*. This was the first step in his long-desired plan to establish himself in British circles. The next, inevitably, was to pursue his intention of finding the right kind of Englishwoman.

Gabrielle and Boy began to drift apart again. While he made incursions into upper-class English life, she made her own independent path into a new circle of friends, including Jean Cocteau, the actress Cécile Sorel, and the wife of a Spanish painter, Misia Sert, who was to become a life-long friend and support. With her new bobbed hairdo, Gabrielle was becoming a fashionable personality in her own right.

She was not the creator of the new cropped haircut, though in later years Coco made up wild stories about how she created the vogue. It was a dancer, one of those enchanting creatures of the theatrical world, Caryathis, who was the first to cast off long locks. Caryathis ran a dance studio in Montmartre, teaching an expressive form of modern dance, in the mould of Isadora Duncan. For a while Gabrielle kept up her fantasy of a stage life, by taking dancing lessons under her aegis. But finally she had to recognise that dance and song were not for her – apart from a lack of talent, she had a fashion business that gave her a substantial income.

These were her formative years, her university of the world, where she learned about art, music and drama. Misia Sert was a natural educator – correcting Gabrielle's provincial mode of speaking, so that she fitted even better into these opinionated, stylish circles. Gabrielle was a quick learner, and wanted nothing better than to disguise her origins. Rustic expressions and a common accent were entirely out of place now that she belonged to Paris by her own efforts.

José María Sert, Misia's husband, painted frescoes, working in elaborate colorations, intense detail, even applying gold leaf. The cartoonist and satirist Sem, a good friend of Gabrielle's, once said of his work and the large scale of his creations, 'Yes, but they shrink. . . .' Coco said of Sert, 'One felt intelligent when one listened to him.' A Catalan, he knew Salvador Dali, whom Gabrielle later entertained at her villa on the south coast. But in Paris at this period, the best place to see and be seen, where the Serts and Gabrielle went often, was the famous nightclub and rendezvous of the newest talents: Le Boeuf sur Le Toit.

While Gabrielle played and polished her manners, Boy Capel was pursuing a double victory. First he clinched a major contract with Clemenceau to supply the war industries with coal, and secondly he proposed and was accepted by none less than the daughter of a peer, Diana Wyndham, whose father was Baron Ribblesdale. She was a war widow, a nurse, and appealed to his protective instincts.

What a contrast then for him to return to Paris and find Gabrielle glittering with success and altogether seductive, the irresistible new being, 'Coco'. The affair revived with its old ardour, until Boy was finally forced to reveal the truth about his forthcoming marriage.

It is a measure of the depth of feeling Gabrielle had for Boy Capel that she allowed herself to move from the heart of Paris to a new apartment on the Quai de Tokio, accepting any kind of role in Boy's life, even that of discreet, secluded mistress.

Once again the Germans drew near to the French capital, a new and dreadful offensive. Enormous losses to the French army, the decimation of the once-brave cavalry that Gabrielle knew so intimately, and appalling casualties among the

Coco bought herself a Rolls-Royce to celebrate her success

allies followed. But by the autumn of 1918, the Americans were beginning to turn the tide. Boy's wedding could no longer be postponed and he went to Scotland to be married from Baron Ribblesdale's castle. Gabrielle heard the news just as the Great War at last reached its end.

Even Gabrielle's flight to yet another hideaway outside Paris did not bring the end of her torment. As soon as a decent period of time had elapsed (during which his wife gave birth to their first daughter), Boy Capel returned to Paris, sought her out, and re-established the love affair as if his marriage meant nothing.

But this time, the end was near. Gabrielle had become more and more isolated, a feeling in no way reduced by flinging herself at many, many men during Boy's defection. Then there was the loss of her personal allies. The devoted Antoinette chose to marry a Canadian pilot. A short disastrous liaison, it ended when Antoinette fled with a lover to South America and died a little over a year later of a virulent form of influenza. Then Boy Capel's sister, Bertha, stupidly allowed herself to be inveigled into a 'white marriage' for money, a route through life which the passionate Gabrielle found loathsome. Not to have love in a marriage was unthinkable to her. Adrienne was still involved with the son of a Baron.

It was the second Christmas after the war's end, 1919. Boy Capel set out from Paris, by car, with his chauffeur, Mansfield, heading for the south of France where his wife was waiting for him. Just outside Cannes, a tyre on the car burst, the car careered off the road and went up in flames. Boy was trapped and died in the conflagration.

Gabrielle was brought the news by a close personal friend, Léon de Laborde, one of the old set from Royallieu. He was never to forget the fact that Gabrielle did not shed a single tear, but went to pack her things at once. They drove all through the following day until they reached the south coast in the middle of the following night, too late to see the body, already nailed in its coffin. Gabrielle chose not to go to the funeral. Instead, she insisted on going to the scene of the crash, where Boy's car, a write-off, still lay in a heap at the side of the road. Only here did her iron control give way and she cried at last, giving vent to all her grief. She was in her prime: thirty-six years old, rich and famous. With the death of Boy all her hopes of enduring happiness in love vanished. From now on, Gabrielle would only have 'affairs'.

In keeping with his unorthodox, bold style of life, Boy Capel made his liaisons perfectly public to the world after his death. In his will he named both Gabrielle Chanel and another mistress, an Italian countess, who were each to receive forty thousand pounds. The bulk of the estate was divided between his relatives, his wife and his two children – for at the time of his death, Diana Capel was expecting their second child.

RUE CAMBON

The strength of passion Gabrielle Chanel felt for Boy Capel was limitless. He had made her the woman she was, a metamorphosis for which she was intensely grateful, but which meant little to her without his presence, however erratic, to enjoy the results. He had given her the courage to build up an empire, but he reduced her to enslavement in her love for him. Or at least, that was how Gabrielle experienced the effects of his love. Money made no difference, whether it was her own hard-earned money or the generous remembrance of his will. What was material security without companionship? How she must have hated knowing she had lost him to a proper English wife, that, in the end, the social gap between them made him unattainable always.

Gabrielle often claimed that her love of all things English dated from the days when Boy took her into the best houses, where she was accepted without question. What she failed to realise was that as a foreigner, she was beyond their recognition – they could perfectly well afford to be kind to someone outside their circle. However, when it came to marriage, to joining the ruling élite, Boy and the class he fought so hard to belong to closed ranks and shut her out. This realisation seemed not to dawn on her; her ego, her ambition, blinded her to any limitations of her hopes. In that lay her success and her dissatisfaction with life. Gabrielle's tragedy lay in this unconscious belief that her will to love and be loved by the most powerful, the richest men of her time, would succeed. It doomed her to failure in relationships from the start. Her lovers were always unavailable men.

Needless to say her professional life was inexorably growing in success. A French fabric manufacturer, Rodier, introduced her to an unpopular textile, knitted jersey. Once before a *femme fatale* had adopted this clinging, sensuous material as her trademark: Lillie Langtry, whose home, the island of Jersey, gave the fabric its name. Just as Gabrielle introduced men's shirts, pullovers and smocks from the boutique in Deauville, she now revolutionised fashion in the Twenties by upgrading jersey from an underwear fabric to a daywear mode. She made simple tunic dresses that fell just short of the ankle. One of the first models was made for her actress friend, Gabrielle Dorziat, a friend from the days of Royallieu, and one of the first French stars to model Chanel hats for the pages of fashion magazines. The new outfit consisted of a tailored navy blue dress with a cardigan jacket sporting a little fur collar – rabbit, supplied, by one of those niceties of history, by a man who later became a considerable couturier in his own right (and a rival she treated with vehemence), Jacques Heim.

It must be admitted that, like many other women designers, Gabrielle created styles in her own image – she was by far the best exponent of her 'look', and readily admitted that she designed the simple loose lines because she had too little figure, too little bust to compete with the currently praised voluptuousness of Parisienne cocottes. Madeleine Vionnet's draped, bias-cut dresses were more the thing for women with busts and bottoms. Women who liked high-style, formally tailored clothes could go to Captain Molyneux or the House of Worth. Gabrielle's clothes filled a gap in the market. Many ample-hipped women were charmed into believing that they looked as lithe and youthful as she did in her own designs. Not always with success. Gabrielle Chanel's revolution was to create a line, a look, remote from the Belle Epoque exoticisms of Paul Poiret, still the reigning king of couture. In fact Poiret once said, 'We ought to have been on guard against that boyish head. It was going to give us every kind of shock. . . .' He also said, in less generous mood, that in his day, women looked beautiful and architectural, like the figures on the prows of great ships. Under Chanel's influence, they had become 'little underfed *télégraphistes*'. However, he ended his days in penury; Gabrielle, hers, as one of the richest women in the world. Her only other serious rival during the Twenties was Jean Patou; both designers claimed to have invented 'separates', mix-and-match wardrobes, of the utmost simplicity, and both realised fairly early in their careers that the future for couture had to be found in designing with the American woman in mind, not merely the French, for that was where the big money was. Patou imported lanky American girls as his mannequins; within weeks Gabrielle was poaching them away with the promise of higher salaries. She was not averse to some fairly sharp practices. So it is no coincidence that Chanel's first entry into fashion pages and fashion history lay with the illustration of one of her chemise dresses in American *Harper's Bazaar*, as early as 1916.

This was the year that Gabrielle moved further along the rue Cambon to larger premises at number 31 – the address that is still the centre of the Chanel empire. On Boy's death she flung herself into her work with a despairing determination. She also moved from the suburban villa where she had received the news of his fatal accident, to a new rural location, the villa of 'Bel Respiro' set in the trees of Garches.

Friends helped to distract her, to lift her from her grief. The most valued of these was Misia. She was a perpetual *saloniste*, living for a time at the Hôtel Meurice, surrounded by her oriental fans, her iris-blue butterflies, baroque figures of negroes, and Venetian glass ornaments. Misia Sert was one of those women whose talent for friendship, for recognising originality or brilliance, makes them precious in their circle and ubiquitous in the pages of artists' biographies. Jean Cocteau described her best in an article in *Paris-Midi*:

'One should honour those sincere, sparkling women who live in the shadow of the men of their epoch and who, with the artists' world, through the simple fact that they emanate a radiance more beautiful than necklaces, exercise an occult influence. It is impossible to imagine the gold of José María Sert's ceilings, the sunlit universe of Renoir, of Bonnard, of Vuillard, of Roussel, of Debussy, of Ravel . . . without seeing rise up the silhouette of the young beribboned tiger, the soft and cruel face, like a pink cat, that belongs to Misia. . . .'

She was a pretty, vital, rounded young woman when Gabrielle first met her, already on her third husband. The first was a bohemian Pole, Thadée Natanson; the second a millionaire newspaper owner, Alfred Edwards, and the third, José

Igor Stravinsky, José María Sert, Misia and Coco at the Foire de Paris, 1920

María Sert. She had many other admirers, Vuillard, Diaghilev, Cocteau, Satie among them, but in the end it was her women friends who inspired intimacy and devotion. Misia and Gabrielle were made for each other, if only through their mutual taste for stress and drama.

Coco: 'She came into my life at the moment of my greatest sorrow. Other people's suffering attracted her as certain smells attract bees. We like people for their defects of character and Misia gave me good cause to be fond of her. Misia was only fascinated by what she could not understand – and she understood most things; but she always found me mysterious, so she clung to me desperately, and if we had a row she was soon back, close as ever.'

Through Misia Gabrielle had become acquainted with the artistic and bohemian circles of Paris, for José María Sert was well-connected, an intimate of Serge Diaghilev, who was one of the most important cultural figures of the age, having brought the Ballets Russes to the capital, and having worked with the finest contemporary composers and artists. To know Diaghilev was to know the creative pulse of the time. However, after Boy, Gabrielle was less Misia's hanger-on, and more exploratory, more daring in her social advances.

The Serts took Gabrielle to Venice, as therapy. There she met the great Diaghilev himself, surrounded by his court of admirers. He took little notice of her, but Gabrielle listened well. 'I looked at him, I observed very attentively. Misia was always telling me about him and about music, she fed me on her memories. I enjoyed her very much. And here I was, unnoticed in my corner, but aware of some great drama taking place for Diaghilev.'

The drama was his current project: he was planning a revival of *Le Sacre du Printemps* and was, as usual, desperately short of money. By the time Gabrielle returned to Paris, she had decided on two great artistic gestures. The first was to let Igor Stravinsky and his family live in her villa, Bel Respiro, so that the composer could work in peace. Stravinsky became fairly besotted with Gabrielle for a time, a state of affairs soon perceived by his wife, who abruptly left Garches, on the pretext that the Atlantic air of Biarritz would be better for their children's health. The affair was shortlived, but resulted in Gabrielle's second act of generosity. This was to finance Diaghilev's ballet. She paid 300,000 francs for the staging of *The Rite*, on condition that the donation would remain anonymous. Undoubtedly the main reason for her reticence was that she wanted her brief fling with Stravinsky to remain a secret.

Stravinsky brought the affair to an end by having another fleeting romantic encounter with Genia Nikitina, a well-known singer. It says much for Gabrielle's good heart that she recognised the philanderer in the composer, and did not allow this to affect her good intent. As André Boucourechliev, Stravinsky's biographer explained: '. . . it was in this very Parisian milieu dominated by Chanel and Misia Sert, and in the euphoric atmosphere of successful love affairs (which he was very good at concealing) that Stravinsky, with his accustomed imperturbability, was to complete at Garches one of his most serious and fervently unworldly works: *Symphonies of Wind Instruments.*'

It is intriguing that Gabrielle's support of the arts is the least-known aspect of her varied life, almost as if she did not feel entitled to be a patroness, however much money she made. Perhaps it smacked too much of 'noblesse oblige', which was not the style of a self-made girl from the Cévennes. On the other hand, she had good cause to be self-effacing. The ballerina Vera Sudeikina recalls that after the 1923 production of *Les Noces*, the Singer-sewing-machine heiress, the Princess de Polignac, gave a celebratory party, in her role as benefactress. Vera asked her why Gabrielle Chanel was not invited. 'I don't entertain tradespeople,' was the tart reply. The greatest couturiers, such as Worth or Doucet, would never expect to be greeted by their customers in a public place such as the enclosure at Longchamps. These were the values that Gabrielle knew well, and sought to destroy.

When Gabrielle reflected on her generosity in later years, she explained the matter differently. She went to Diaghilev with her offer of finance behind Misia's back. Even at this successful, mature point in her life, at the age of forty, she did not revel in her own success well enough not to be fearful of causing offence: Misia would be made jealous, because she did not have the funds to help Diaghilev herself.

Curiously, Serge Lifar, a close collaborator with Diaghilev, explained to Gabrielle after the event, 'You gave him (Diaghilev) money and did not ask for anything in return. He didn't understand; that frightened him.' Gabrielle was astonished by this revelation and remembered it with undimmed surprise to the end of her life.

The Venetian trip and the making of new artistic plans cured Gabrielle of her grief about Boy Capel. From Rome she sent orders back to Paris that everything should be cleared from her apartment. Too many memories. On her return she moved into the Hôtel Ritz, which, conveniently, filled the block between the rue Cambon and the place Vendôme – the centre of the world of fashion. She kept with her, from this date, a souvenir from a church in Italy, a statue of St Anthony of Padua, recalling the moment on her travels when she had given up her grief, and started the process of reviving. It stayed with her all her life, together with a small Russian icon Igor Stravinsky gave her in gratitude for her generosity – and for her good grace over their brief liaison.

Back in Paris, Misia continued to enliven Gabrielle's evenings by producing a

stream of interesting visitors: playwrights such as Jean Giraudoux, composers like Erik Satie or Georges Auric, film directors, writers like Raymond Radiguet, tennis champions and boxers too, arriving on the heels of Cocteau, not to mention various Russians of the imperial family.

It was through this circle that Gabrielle met her next grand lover. Paris was well used to the flood of Russian refugees from the Red Revolution. The handsomest young men became gigolos in smart clubs, or worked in antique shops; the less physically attractive became taxi-drivers. Grand Duke Dimitri did not have to sink so low. A cousin of Tsar Nicholas II, he was discovered at Biarritz, a sort of Casablanca of the Twenties where Gabrielle's first *maison de couture* was booming in business. The story goes that the Grand Duke was at a party in the tow of Marthe Davelli, the young opera singer whom Gabrielle had first met in the early days of her friendship with Boy Capel and Etienne Balsan. She was now the star of the Opéra Comique, and always dressed by Chanel.

Russian noblemen are expensive playthings. Before long Marthe had handed the Grand Duke on to Gabrielle, who lodged him at Bel Respiro, with his faithful valet, Piotr, in attendance. Piotr was everything a romantic Hollywood film would make of a servant of a Romanov, a hairy, bear-like man who chose exile with his master (implicated in the plot to assassinate Rasputin), rather than live in revolutionary Russia. Grand Duke Dimitri had experienced all the horrors of war, intrigue and imprisonment it is possible to know in twenty-nine years.

Good-looking in a blond, sad-eyed sort of way, immensely tall and exquisitely mannered, Dimitri became devoted to Gabrielle. For the rest of his life he claimed she was his one true love. For Gabrielle, in middle age, eleven years older and sadder than her man, the affair brought consolation and a recovery of her self-esteem. On reflection, Coco was fairly dismissive of the Grand Duke's charms. 'Those Grand Dukes were all the same – they looked marvellous but there was nothing behind. Green eyes, fine hands and shoulders, peace-loving, timorous. They drank so as not to be afraid . . . behind it all – nothing, just vodka and the void.'

Coco's affair with Stravinsky inspired one of his most serious works,
Symphonies of Wind Instruments

CHANEL NO. 5

The greatest mark of Gabrielle's recovery from the tragedy of Boy Capel's death was the energy with which she embarked on a whole new venture – the creation of her first perfume, No. 5.

There are fashions in perfume as there are in clothes. Each era has its favourite smells, a whiff of which evokes instantly the charms and beauties of each succeeding age.

In the Twenties, women were the new consumers. Whole styles of decoration were aimed directly at them for the first time in marketing history. The dearth of servants created the vogue for cocktail cabinets (cocktails themselves arising out of the American necessity to mask the filthy taste of illicit liquor in the days of Prohibition). The cocktail cabinet was introduced to the lounge, while the dressing table became the newest feature of a smart bed or dressing room. It was an altar to beauty, often manufactured with neat little glass trays for Madame's new and entirely acceptable cosmetics in pots and flasks, artificial jewels, and fancy perfume bottles.

Poiret had been the first to market scents in his personally-designed flacons. His creations had exotic names, such as 'Chinese Night' or 'Lucrezia Borgia'. Glass itself was the most popular material for interior design in the Twenties. Combined with stainless steel, the new plastics, chrome or mirrored surfaces, nothing captured the brittle brilliance of the age more aptly.

The originality of Gabrielle's special scent was not of course her achievement alone. No. 5 made perfume history and was the final product of years of painstaking research by a master 'nose' or perfumer, Ernest Beaux. It was unique because of its composition. Before No. 5 all perfumes were made from formulas based on natural scents: combined like a harmonious musical chord, with base notes for long-lasting qualities, *corps* or body notes to give a rounded character to the creation, and top notes, also called the *tête* or *départ*, for an instant, ephemeral attraction when first applied. Since the middle of the nineteenth century, chemists had been working to synthesise the natural essences of perfumes, that is, to manufacture in the laboratory the scent of the rose, carnation, lavender, and so on. The aim was to stabilise the supply of ingredients, and to enlarge the manufacturing potential of perfumes, by lowering the cost of the materials.

Gabrielle felt that she had changed women's habits in dress and accessories, but she wanted to make a 'couture' perfume, something that reflected the essence of her style. This was an extraordinary concept, as modern in its way as the work of the abstract painters she knew, like Picasso and Dali. She once said, 'A woman should smell like a woman, not a rose. . . .' It was a compulsion, in the sense that cleanliness was almost an obsession with her, and her sense of smell was extraordinarily over-developed. Coco used to say that when she was given a posy, she could smell the odour of the hands that picked the flowers. She judged people and places by their smell, cleanliness or sweetness being seen as a positive virtue in anyone she liked or loved. She recalled the *grandes cocottes* of her youth, how they smelled clean and fresh, even if only of soap, and in that they exercised an enormous allure. Upper-class women, on the other hand, were often a little 'high' in a derogatory sense of the word. If Gabrielle had done nothing else in her life, she would have earned a notable place in social history for her success in understanding the art of perfumery, and bringing it to new heights of attraction.

'I wanted to give women a perfume that was artificial,' she claimed, 'exactly in the way that a dress is artificial, that is, man-made. I'm an artisan in dressmaking . . . I don't want the smell of rose, or lily or the valley. I want a perfume that is a composition.' It was a comparatively small step to train her sense of smell like a professional perfumer.

Gabrielle went to visit Ernest Beaux at Grasse, the capital of the perfume world. He became aware at once that she had a vision of something completely new in perfumery, and might be exactly the person with whom his dream might be realised. She worked hard at picking up the craft of perfume composition, so much so that Beaux recognised in her the innate talent of a master of his métier. He made up about eight to ten samples, and Gabrielle selected the fifth (according to Pierre Galante who covered her business enterprises in his book, *Les Années Chanel*). The samples were made up of chemically synthesised aldehydes, the first in a long line of 'green' perfumes, that smelt of themselves, and in no way imitated a perfume in nature. In thinking of a name, Gabrielle stuck to the chance of her choice – the fifth sample became Chanel No. 5. Ernest Beaux advised her that the perfume contained more than twenty-four ingredients, but this did not deter her. The more expensive it was, the more desirable it would be. She already knew from the sale of couture dresses, how much the public will pay for the excitement of a luxury in short supply.

Unlike Poiret, Gabrielle had the vision to see right to the logical end of her projects. Poiret's perfumes had been sold under the name of 'Rosine', the christian name of one of his daughters. So they never capitalised on his personal fame. Gabrielle, in contrast, saw the new scent as a way of keeping her professional identity valuable, and of attracting new clients. (In fact, simultaneous with the launching of Chanel No. 5, the firm of Coty, for whom Beaux had previously worked, offered to buy all the perfumes of 'Rosine', and to launch them as rivals. Poiret, as always unable to overcome his resistance to commerce, refused.)

Gabrielle's manner of establishing her latest project was typically cunning (and owed quite a lot to watching her father at work in the market square). She took samples back to Paris, and offered them as little gifts to her best clients. 'Oh, you liked it did you? Sell you more? Oh no, I couldn't do that, it was just something I picked up from a man in Grasse, I don't even remember his name now. . . .'

Pampered and disappointed, her clients were more determined than ever to have their way, and Gabrielle could report back to Beaux that she had an ever-increasing demand.

A great personal friend of Gabrielle's, the Russian-born but English by marriage, socialite and actress, Iya, Lady Abdy, described how Gabrielle worked at this

Chanel No. 5 looked expensive and chic, in a simple flacon

time. 'Her egotism was extreme. Her energy fantastic. She'd decide to do something and follow her idea up to the ultimate conclusion. She put every ounce of her energy into a project, to realise it and make it succeed. When she began to be interested in perfumery, she wanted to learn everything about the subject – composition, manufacture, the lot. She asked for advice, naturally, from a few people, and managed to acquire the best chemist, one of the greatest men of Grasse, but in the end, it was Chanel, and her alone, who made the decisions.'

In 1923, Gabrielle asked Théophile Bader, the owner of Galeries Lafayette stores, to give her some help in launching her perfumes nationally. He in turn introduced her to two brothers, the Wertheimers, who ran one of the biggest perfume companies in France, Bourjois. Pierre Wertheimer and Gabrielle came to a lamentably simple agreement (unfortunate in that it left plenty of room for mistrust and abuse). The Wertheimers would set up a company to manufacture and distribute all of Gabrielle's perfumes, and she would hold 200 shares worth 500 francs each, that is ten per cent of the capital invested. She would also own ten per cent of all branches set up abroad. For her part she was to hand over all her formulas and manufacturing processes.

Almost at once there were problems. 'Parfums Chanel' brought out a cleansing cream under her name. Gabrielle thought she had only agreed to the making and selling of perfumes through the company. The battle took five years through the courts, and in the end she lost the case. Several protective clauses were added to the agreement, safeguarding the quality of anything marketed under her name, prohibiting Gabrielle from making or distributing perfumes independently, but giving her the right of veto over any product that was suggested by the partners.

In succeeding years Parfums Chanel brought out several other perfumes, Bois des Iles, Gardenia and Cuir de Russie, No. 19 and No. 22 but, although their sales were excellent, none ever reached the heights of No. 5.

Coco advised: 'Spray it on wherever you expect to be kissed – any woman who goes to excess in perfuming herself has no future because she will only offend her friends and admirers.' Much later, she regretted these words: 'I shouldn't have said that, because old women, the ones who don't get kissed any more, will stop buying it.' A bitter remark from a woman who never felt she had passed the kissing age herself.

In keeping with the unfussy style of her dress designs, Chanel's No. 5 was a new departure in marketing by being sold in a simple square-cut, clear glass container. It looked expensively chic and simple – a complete change from the elaborate coloured glass flacons of the past, with moulded flowers or pearlised finish. The plain container was a statement: 'No more pretty bottles, mere decoration. This perfume is an essential item.' And so, to judge by the sales, it was.

Satisfied, if not secure in the success of her new venture, Gabrielle spent an idyllic summer with Grand Duke Dimitri at a villa at Moulleau, near Arcachon, in comparative seclusion. Friends of her lover's occasionally visited, while Dimitri's Piotr and Gabrielle's manservant Joseph were in constant attendance. The couple went fishing, walking, or played with Gabrielle's entourage of dogs.

Not for long. Paris summoned her back to work. Due to Dimitri's influence, several White Russians found themselves employed as *vendeuses*, or sales assistants, and *essayeuses*, or fitters, at the rue Cambon salon. Gabrielle herself left the organisation of the workrooms to the various heads of departments, but a few titled ladies, in the jobs where they came into contact with the clientèle, added definite cachet to her salon. Coco remembered: 'It was the Russians who taught women it isn't degrading to work. My grand duchesses used to knit.' A stream of titled, exiled women began to fill the salon, patronising these less fortunate refugees from the Russian Revolution, much to Gabrielle's delight. There was a certain satisfaction in employing women of high birth – Gabrielle had a love-hate relationship with the élite. Her best revenge for her undistinguished background was to make the wealthy come to her salon, and pay through the nose for their clothes.

In the words of Mme Hélène de Leusse, who worked for some eighteen months as *directrice* of the Chanel boutique: 'What would you expect – she was from a very very simple background. She had hardly received any real education. It was Balsan who put her on the first rung of the ladder. But at the outset, she was completely without culture. She improved herself little by little because she surrounded herself with intelligent people and then of course, she was intelligent herself. . . . In my opinion she was quite a snob, and snobbery helped her a great deal . . . she had a Machiavellian side, if you like.'

Horror of her own humble beginnings showed itself in another characteristic. Gabrielle hardly ever went into her workrooms, not out of lack of interest, but as if mere contact with the struggling little seamstresses would drag her back down to their level. She was utterly impossible as an employer, expecting anyone to work overtime when she saw fit, making mannequins stand in front of her for hours, while she ruminated and adjusted a garment. An occasional act of generosity could be offered to former employees: she once helped a worker who had gone blind to be rehabilitated.

Occasionally she sent younger girls on holidays to Mimizan where she now had a property, without deducting the holiday time from their pay. In general, her mannequins were paid a derisory sum. Gabrielle would reject any criticism of their pay by saying baldly, working for Chanel gave them the chance to find the richest lovers. (She was not out of step with all the other couturiers of her time,

Chanel. 1922 – Roubachka, black crêpe-de-chine

who also paid their girls badly.) Gabrielle had been brought up with old peasant values: a boss was a boss and an employee did whatever he or she was told. Keeping company with autocratic individuals, both in society and in the world of the arts, did little to alter her native philosophy. However, in spite of her demands, most former employees reminisce about their time with the House of Chanel as the most worthwhile and inspiring era of their lives, because of her instinctive, totally unswerving dedication to beauty.

How did Gabrielle Chanel manage her empire, and yet take time off to conduct her love affairs? The structure of a couture house lends itself to both requirements. Gabrielle would do the designing, most often by word of mouth rather than in drawn sketches. Her commands would be passed on to heads of workrooms, who would produce a prototype for her scrutiny. Gabrielle would then adjust or alter the basic garment, and then the 'model' would be shown to the public in her seasonal collections. Gabrielle might need to be on hand for the launch of each new group of designs, but the day-to-day running of the couture houses in Paris and Biarritz could easily be delegated, in all frankness, to *vendeuses*, *essayeuses*, and *premières* (heads of workrooms) more skilled in dressmaking than she was herself. Gabrielle was primarily a stylist, in tune with the requirements of her time; secondly an astute businesswoman, who knew how to flatter and win the clients most prominent in society at the time and, lastly, a hard taskmaster of her employees.

Gabrielle was not the only designer of the mid-Twenties to introduce Russian ethnic influences into her designs: she created embroidered borders to hems, wide-sleeved shirts like a peasant's belt blouse, and fur-trimmed collars for a whole series of suits worthy of a latter-day Anna Karenina. The Grand Duke's sister, Grand Duchess Maria, was put in charge of a new embroidery workshop for Chanel. As Gabrielle grew older and less romantic, she used any encounter for best profit. She was not entirely hard or unscrupulous, but made harshly aware, by circumstances, that her work was her destiny, not the current man in her life, whoever he might be.

The Grand Duke was sweet but no more than a year-long diversion. Gabrielle's relationship with him ended on his marriage to an American heiress, Audrey Emery, in Biarritz. He followed in the longstanding tradition among defunct European aristocrats of selling his title for a secure future in the New World.

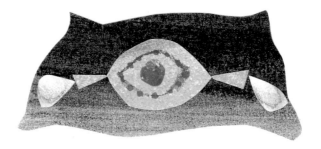

Coco filled her rooms with coromandel screens for an exotic privacy

FAUBOURG
ST - HONORE

With the end of her Russian affair, and the death of Marie, her faithful servant Joseph's wife, the villa of Bel Respiro became no longer a peaceful retreat, but a burdensome property too far from Paris and evoking too many memories of good times now past. In Paris, Gabrielle moved to grander quarters, a dignified, gloomy apartment in the faubourg St Honoré, one floor of a *hôtel particulier* that she leased from Count Pillet-Will. It was only a short walk from her House in the rue Cambon, and the same street where her fading rival, Paul Poiret, had held so many glittering parties. Here, Joseph ruled as major domo and Gabrielle filled the high-ceilinged, long-windowed rooms with the opulent furnishings favoured and suggested by her friends Misia and José-María Sert. The gardens reached as far as the avenue Gabriel, not very far from the Champs Elysées. With Misia on hand to give advice, Gabrielle filled her rooms with coromandel screens (she could not alter the green and gold painted walls as the house had historic value). A favourite colour scheme of beige, white and *tête de nègre* was carried throughout the rooms. Huge Louis XIV chairs of old wood or covered with white velvet upholstery filled the spaces. The terrace could be seen from the windows of the salon and beyond that a fountain in the lawn and century-old trees. White floral displays filled all the rooms – her favourite colour for flowers.

The coromandel screens became legendary; Coco installed them wherever she lived from now on. 'Lacquer's my element. It doesn't hit you in the eye. I've bought thirty-two screens in my time, and I've given a lot of them away, but there's enough left to cover my house. . . .'

The apartment became the rendezvous of all Gabrielle's artistic Parisian circle. One of Misia's real talents lay in music. She played the piano superbly – well enough to enchant composers like Stravinsky. Diaghilev visited frequently, and occasionally the painter Picasso. 'Music. People lay on settees and I discovered art. . . . With those people you were never bored. They didn't talk art, thank God, they created it, which isn't the same thing. . . .'

A new lover appeared in Gabrielle's life, one so removed from her previous men that he touched an altogether different set of responses in her. This was the poet, Pierre Reverdy. A small man with a mass of jet black hair, and fine eyes, he had the dark skin of a southerner. In fact his family came from Languedoc, the southernmost part of the Cévennes. His father had once been a wine-grower whose business collapsed in the first decade of the century. A curious coincidence, in that Gabrielle in later years often upgraded her costermonger bar-tender father into a wine-merchant.

So Reverdy had experienced hardship in his childhood, and knew the same country values that Gabrielle had imbibed and tried to suppress. In *En Vrac*, a collection of his sayings, he commented on family life in a way that Gabrielle would with ease endorse:

'Brothers who are enemies, brothers and sisters who are enemies, I think that is entirely normal. Too much complicity in the spirit and in feelings about this shared issue of parenthood – perhaps in all issues of kin – is a little similar to a kind of incest.'

Compare Coco: 'I don't like the family. You're born in it, not of it. I don't know anything more terrifying than the family.'

But there were two major obstacles to the relationship. One was Reverdy's obsession with the ascetic, religious life, the other, his devoted wife, Henriette.

Henriette dated far back to Reverdy's first days in Paris before the Great War, when he lived in Montmartre and worked as a proofreader for daily newspapers and small printers. Once Henriette worked for a fashion designer, as a pattern cutter, but gave up her job to devote herself full time to marriage, and looking after Pierre. Many artists thought her beautiful and wanted to paint her, but she never would agree to sit for anyone.

Reverdy had volunteered for the army as soon as war was declared but was discharged as medically unfit in 1916. He then launched a small but highly respected literary review, called *Nord-Sud*. He moved in bohemian circles, met Juan Gris and Picasso, published the thoughts of the Dadaist Tristan Tzara and the Surrealist André Breton, and used illustrations by Léger, Braque and Derain.

His life became linked with Gabrielle's through Misia, of course. She described him in her short autobiographical volume, *Misia par Misia*: 'I first knew him in 1920. Quite young, he already seemed fundamentally shattered by life. He was a curious mixture of deeply Christian humility and violent revolt; one was almost physically aware of the permanent torture of his soul.'

Misia loved the little review, *Nord-Sud*, proclaimed it to her friends and helped Reverdy in every way possible. Gabrielle's first encounter with him took place in 1917. A year later his review folded but not before he had become something of a name, and found a publisher for his poetry.

When he took up with Gabrielle in 1921, the conflicts and inconsistencies of his existence were driving him to distraction. He loved the good life, but he was equally drawn to a life of asceticism and contemplation. He would spend days with Gabrielle, then suddenly disappear to his garret in Montmartre, overcome

with remorse at his infidelity and with distaste for the opulence of his life in the faubourgs, the bars and restaurants of the city. As he wrote: 'If one had no need of anything, how easy it would be not to need anyone.'

Gabrielle adored Reverdy. His ambivalence became a challenge, his gloom a destructive force that she sought to overcome. Perhaps she was more able to be her true self with Pierre than with any other man. But in the end, she knew she could not hold on to him. Besides all his goodness, he too was a womaniser, incapable of fidelity.

Gabrielle's friends saw the impossible nature of the relationship. Paul Morand the writer described her as a 'friend of lost causes'. Gabrielle was once more ensnared in an impossible liaison, pitting her wits and her will against a reluctant man. Reverdy would complain: 'On the whole, women lack a sense of humour, perhaps because they take love too seriously. And in life, just as in art, alas, it shows through.'

One by one he began shedding all his artistic and literary acquaintances. For in 1921, Reverdy found the answer to his spiritual and moral dilemma by converting to Catholicism. He became influenced by the writings of a French philosopher, Jacques Maritain – as were many intellectuals of the time, including Cocteau and Maurice Sachs, who was the catalyst for Reverdy's conversion. It was not a rapid or direct progress towards spiritual salvation. At times he would revive his love of life and return to Gabrielle. He wrote long, agonised letters on his desire for isolation, a purer kind of existence. 'Oh God, solitude,' he once wrote, 'yes, but only after you cut off my head and tear my heart from me – not before.'

By 1924 the process of separation was complete. Reverdy severed his connection with Gabrielle and retreated to a cottage near the monastery of Solesmes, outside Paris, with Henriette. Gabrielle had to accept his choice: she had lost.

In later days Gabrielle spoke only with the utmost affection and respect for Reverdy. His love for her lingered in her memory as a fine and precious thing. She struggled with his despair because she knew that bleakness of mind herself, better than anyone else of his circle. He wrote loving dedications in many of his works to her, not only during the years of their affair, but for the rest of his life. She for her part had the deepest respect for his work, and minded desperately that he never received the recognition due to him for his excellence, in his life or by posthumous reappraisal. 'Once you've started on *Le Gant de crin* . . . I could give up everything because I haven't lived that life. Just to have written a few phrases that give food for dreams. . . . He was severe only with himself – for everyone else, he melted.'

In philosophical mood towards the end of her life, Coco spoke in words that

Coco's lover, the poet Pierre Reverdy, was torn between the good life and one of asceticism and contemplation

echoed this most fragile and intense of loves: 'Give up one's soul to God – I like that expression. . . . What remains of us is what we've thought and loved in life. The life one leads is unimportant. The life one dreams, that's the great existence, because one goes on with it after death.'

For his part, Reverdy was inspired by her courage and independence. These words from *Livre de Mon Bord* show his sympathy for women's predicament: 'One must give to women all the liberty and freedoms that their nature, their intelligence and their faculties require – a freedom so great that men, in whom women only admire strength in general, would themselves at last be liberated.'

There were links of a very special and private nature between Pierre and Gabrielle: they both had a strong sense of solitariness, a gritty, self-imposed struggle with creativity, a life-long battle with the essential emptiness of existence (even though their solutions were at times so different) and a peasant contempt for those who sought public acclaim and status. Reverdy wrote, 'I know all about the vainglory of posthumous honours, but all the same, I can't help thinking that real glory is a cloak of light which only fits well on a corpse measured up just for it.' His thoughts are finely expressed in a way that translation cannot recapture. (Translation was once defined as looking at the back side of a tapestry; one sees the colours and the pattern, the craft, but not the splendour of the outer side.) About creativity, a subject he discussed with Gabrielle very often, he was of the opinion: 'The privilege of the artist who works with material things lies in the fact that in a debauched world that is intellectually empty, he continues to think with his hands . . . the eye is the most implacable of the senses, the one that lights upon and seeks to dominate most firmly, most clearly, the task that is set the artist.' It reads like a portrait of Gabrielle Chanel at work, especially in that word, 'implacable'.

Gabrielle kept all of Reverdy's work in first edition, a large number of his manuscripts, and his letters. In many of his works, she underlined or ticked passages that held a resonance for her. She was not religious in the way that Reverdy tried to be, struggling with orthodox Catholicism. At times she considered she had no faith at all, in the conventional sense, but a belief in some sort of other dimension, a continuance of life's energy beyond this world. She explained this as springing from her insecurity, her wish that there was something more, including happiness, to come to all after death.

MONTMARTRE

During the years Gabrielle spent with Reverdy, her growing friendships with artists led her to explore new areas of creativity. Picasso had by now become an intimate, sleeping at her apartment from time to time when he knew his one home would be empty, for he had a hatred of being alone. In 1922 he was involved in the production of a Greek tragedy, *Antigone*, adapted by Jean Cocteau. This was to be staged by one of the most successful theatre companies of Paris, the Atelier of the Théâtre de Montmartre, established by Charles Dullin, the lover of Caryathis, once Chanel's dancing teacher and inspiration.

For the first time Chanel agreed to design the costumes, and Cocteau was fulsome in his praise of her. 'I asked Mademoiselle Chanel for the costumes because she is the greatest designer of our day and I do not see Oedipus' daughters being badly dressed.' Gabrielle herself explained her premise with typical brevity: 'Greece is wool, not silk. Men and women dressed in wool.'

Charles Dullin himself played the part of Creon, the playwright Antonin Artaud (later to be famous for his theatre of cruelty), Tiresias, and a Greek actress Genica Athanasiou, the principal role of Antigone. Picasso's settings were painted in shades of terracotta and brown with ionic pillars and classical draperies. The soldiers' shields and the masks of the chorus had an archaic simplicity that suggested pagan forces. But of all the distinguished talents involved in the production, Gabrielle's was generally regarded as the most successful, a subtle blending of the authentic with the spectacular. Predictably certain classical features found their way into her couture collections in 1922, draped jersey dresses, Greek fretted key motifs and similar scorched-earth colours. But Gabrielle, who was probably the first couturier to drape jersey in the twentieth century, left the development of classically draped gowns to the one great exponent, the couturier Alix, later known as Mme Grès.

Cocteau's next extravaganza was created in collaboration with Serge Diaghilev, with whom Gabrielle was now familiar. To work for the Ballets Russes was a tremendous distinction, but one that involved perils. Gabrielle was caught daily between two vast egos, like Scilla and Charybdis, as the new work progressed. *Le Train Bleu* was to be a radical departure, altogether modern and comic, in contrast to the classical ballet repertoire. Darius Milhaud was commissioned to write the score, another radical choice on Diaghilev's part, as the composer's music was known to be serious and complex. But Milhaud was a professional, and highly adaptable. Perhaps unsurprisingly he completed the work in less than three weeks. He later recalled: '*Le Train Bleu* was an operetta without words.

When Diaghilev asked me to do the music for Cocteau's scenario, which was light, frivolous and gay, in the manner of Offenbach, he knew quite well that I would not be able to go in for my usual kind of music which he did not like. . . .'

Other collaborators were less amenable. Bronislava Nijinska, sister of Diaghilev's most famous dancer, Nijinsky, was appointed as the choreographer, adding a third difficult temperament to the enterprise. Classically trained in Russia, she had a challenging task to create the modern dance, which involved sea-side scenes, golfers, tennis players and playboys. She hated the milieu these characters inhabited, having worked with discipline all her life. Besides that Nijinska could not speak French, which hampered her in conveying her artistic objections to Cocteau.

'Le Train Bleu' was the name of the train that ran from the north coast to Paris then on to the south coast, and the piece was meant to be a satire on modern mores. As Diaghilev described: '. . . the first point about *Le Train Bleu* is that there is no blue train in it. This being the age of speed, it has already reached its destination and disembarked its passengers. These are to be seen on a beach which does not exist, in front of a casino which exists still less. Overhead passes an aeroplane which you cannot see. And the plot represents nothing. Yet when it was presented for the first time in Paris, everybody was unaccountably seized with the desire to take the Blue Train to Deauville and perform refreshing exercises.'

Gabrielle's costumes were utterly contemporary, including bathing costumes of the type she sold to her customers at Deauville, white tennis outfits that were provocative and demure, like those worn by Suzanne Lenglen, the French tennis

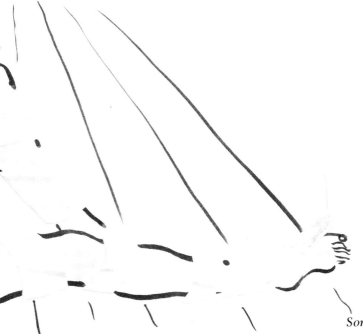

Some of Chanel's designs for Cocteau's productions of Le Train Bleu *(1924),* Antigone *(1923) and* Oedipus Rex *(1937)*

star, including long white stockings. The men wore plus-fours and knitted sweaters in the elegant style of the Duke of Windsor.

Cocteau wanted a kind of super-realism, a hard-edged mixture of satire, pantomime, operetta and documentary. Nijinska, fresh from the success of her previous original ballet choreography, *Les Biches*, disagreed, preferring a more controlled, stylised presentation.

The only people involved in the work who did not display excessive temperament were the dancers. Anton Dolin, a handsome young Englishman, took the part of Beau Gosse, a beach Adonis. The golf player was danced by Woizikowsky, a Polish dancer who had the required lithe limbs for the role. Sokolova, in real life Hilda Munnings, the first English ballerina to join Diaghilev's company, had the role of Perlouse, and Nijinska herself danced the leading figure of the tennis player.

Dress rehearsals can be a nightmare, and *Le Train Bleu* was no exception. Cocteau and Nijinska countermanded each other while the dancers grew confused. Gabrielle's costumes were pronounced unwearable – in movement they rode up or drooped down, giving unattractive lines. Matters were not helped by a lack of heating back-stage and on-stage. 'The dancers came on-stage in Chanel's bathing costumes, some of which had not been tried on before, and the sight of shivering dancers in their scanty, ill-fitting garments was absurd and tragic.' wrote Boris Kochno, Diaghilev's private secretary, later one of the artistic directors of the company. 'Diaghilev fled to the last row of the balcony. He felt utterly powerless to remedy the disaster and asked which other ballets could be substituted for *Le Train Bleu* at this last moment.'

The entire company struggled on through the day, reworking the choreography, while Gabrielle tore apart her costumes and recreated them on more balletic lines. Sokolova remembered later Gabrielle's attention to detail: she promised to think up accessories for the role of Perlouse. 'For the evening performance I found on my dressing table the first of the large pearl stud earrings which were soon to be seen everywhere. They were very smart, but so heavy that they pulled at my ears.'

By curtain up *Le Train Bleu* was transformed and Diaghilev had a dazzling success with which to launch his 1924 season.

Gabrielle's costumes were judged to be totally apposite to the piece, capturing the febrile elegance of the society they characterised. In subsequent years she designed many more wardrobes for Jean Cocteau's theatrical events. In 1928 she provided some costumes for a ballet created by George Balanchine, with music by Stravinsky: *Apollon Musagète*. The sets were designed by André Bauchant. Kochno recorded: 'As for costumes Bauchant confessed he was incapable of designing them so Diaghilev copied Apollo's tunic from the costume of a figure in one of Bauchant's mythological compositions and he dressed the three muses in muslin tissues; later these were replaced by costumes designed by Gabrielle Chanel.' It seems that Gabrielle was willing to be on hand and co-operate in the smallest way without objection. In later years she would barely discuss the subject, or throw any light on her involvement with what was seen afterwards as a dynamic, significant period of French cultural life. Her typical comment was always: 'They were in another world. And anyway, I was only there to do the costumes.' Only there as a craftswoman, not an artist. She would occasionally speak with authority on how designing for the dance was a special process. 'Dancing is not dancing in front of a mirror. You have to forget that. . . . It's very tiring having to throw ballerinas back and forth, you know. . . you have to dance with this' (laying her hand on her solar plexus then suddenly making a gesture of flight) 'and then away.'

On another occasion she added, 'Costume designers work with a pencil: that's art. Fashion designers work with scissors and pins: that's a news item.' Gabrielle had an unfailing sense of realism about what she was and what she was achieving. There were times when she could have seen her work as artistic creation, but there was still too much of the saleswoman in her to allow herself that honour. In spite of acquiring great wealth and many possessions, she never cared too much for material things, and she was never impressed by those who had either. Only pure uncompromising artists, like Reverdy, earned her respect: there was too much of the showman in Jean Cocteau for her to admire him unreservedly.

She shared Reverdy's sentiment: 'Pride is a great handicap when one tries to follow the dirt track that leads to great glory.' Later in her life she became more openly critical of Cocteau, especially when he was lionised by the establishment: '. . . he was well-bred. He never spoke about himself, he was a bourgeois. He had no talent so he listened . . . Just a little tiny bourgeois who tried to steal novelty.'

Just as Reverdy had been scornful of the antics of the Surrealists, and distanced himself from all groups and their manifestos, so Gabrielle was never comfortable in a clique, a group with a label. She was an individual, and would if needs be, live isolated, before she would ever succumb to the comfort of belonging.

In 1929 the Diaghilev ballet danced for the last time in Paris, on 12th June. Gabrielle gave a gala party afterwards; her house in the faubourg Saint Honoré was lit up and a cabaret was provided by an English jazz musician of note, the West Indian Snakehips Johnson, together with black American stars from the 'Blackbirds' revue. Caviar was served from soup tureens, according to the ballet historian, Richard Buckle. It was a wonderful extravagance from a woman who had been snubbed by a princess as a 'mere tradesperson'.

Coco in her mid-forties at the time of her liaison with the Duke of Westminster

EATON HALL

Gabrielle's next love affair put her into another social setting, as far removed from Montmartre as it is possible to be. While holidaying in the South of France in the autumn of 1923, she was introduced to the Duke of Westminster at a party at the Hôtel de Paris. She knew at once who he was – reputedly the richest man in England, with an annual income approximately double the Civil List allowance for his King. She learnt also that he was estranged from his second wife, Violet, and had a considerable reputation as a womaniser. Personally, he made no strong impression on her. He was more of a curiosity, the last of a type – an old-fashioned autocratic aristocrat. But the Duke of Westminster fell for her instantly. He began to press his suit, overwhelming her with expensive presents: baskets of fresh fruit or vegetables delivered by personal courier to Paris (at the bottom of which lay priceless gemstones); fresh fish flown into France from his estates in Scotland. He even secured the help of the Duke of Windsor, bringing him to Gabrielle's home in the rue Cambon, so that he could charm her with his informality, and his obvious willingness to promote his friend the duke's cause. Gabrielle remained wary. She told her friend, Iya, Lady Abdy, that the duke frightened her, and that she had no desire to be yet another conquest. 'I am not one of those women who belong to several men,' she said defiantly. Her very lack of enthusiasm presented the duke with a challenge – there was nothing he liked more than the thrill of the chase.

The Duke of Westminster was after all a Grosvenor – a distinguished family name deriving from the Norman French phrase *gros veneurs* or great hunters, forebears who came to England with and were distantly related to William the Conqueror. Poor 'Bend Or', as he was always known, got his nickname from a horse – a Derby winner for his grandfather, the first Duke of Westminster.

The first duke raised the boy Bend Or when he was orphaned at the age of four. Like the Grand Duke Dimitri, and Gabrielle herself, Bend Or had not known the intimacy of parental affection, although his grandfather indulged him and there was admiration and love between them.

But the old duke was a hard act to follow – a notable peer in the House of Lords, an intimate of Gladstone and the founder of a dazzling line of thoroughbred racing winners at his stables at Eaton Hall that earned him fame and the admiration of all England. He was Master of the Horse to Queen Victoria herself and Derby winner four times. When the old duke died his town of Chester was hung in mourning, flags were lowered to half mast from public buildings all over England and the royal family attended a memorial service for him at Westminster Abbey.

Bend Or was charming, blond, tall, a little plump, very upright and stylish and given to ghastly English humour – pranks. He was the kind of English peer who gives international gossip columnists plenty to say. Lavish with girlfriends, known to have a violent temper that brooked no opposition, amused by stupid games. He changed the engines of his Rolls-Royces every year, but not the bodywork, which would have been needlessly extravagant. 'We're not Argentinians,' he said. Bend Or was a good sailor, a terrific hunter, a lover of dogs, wild flowers and beautiful women. He had many estates in Great Britain, including his principal residence, Eaton Hall in Cheshire, and in France, at Mimizan, besides a regular income from the leases on a goodly slab of central London. All this enabled him to make a show of spending money in the style of his grandfather. But even if he was a man of rather old-fashioned honour, he was no intellectual giant – and a strange choice of lover for Gabrielle Chanel, who was attracted to educated, brilliant men as a rule. She was also now moving in glittering and unusual circles – both the *haut monde* and the *avant garde* of Paris – and was famous enough and sophisticated enough not to be naïvely impressed with a duke's fortune and title. She did not need his fame to give her status; enviably she had enough of her own.

Bend Or never quite achieved his aim, to equal his grandfather's eminence. Various strokes of fate had prevented him from ever finding a calling commensurate with his willpower and abilities. He lived with a sense of frustration, and the burden of comparison with his eminent ancestor. In one of the few accurate and perceptive comments Coco made to her biographer Edmonde Charles-Roux she said, 'To understand what Bend Or was not, you had to know what his grandfather had been.'

Two marriages had produced only two daughters, and a son who died of appendicitis in early childhood. (Compare the first duke, who sired a magnificent total of fifteen offspring . . .)

Perhaps by now Gabrielle was beginning to fear that her love life would never bring the satisfaction she yearned for. That made her cautious, yet at the same time imperious with admirers. She was forty-two, dazzlingly successful, but very much alone at heart. Perhaps, for all her love of things English, the social style, the cut of their cloth, their sportsmanlike mentality, she knew she might never be able to be fully herself within the confines of upper-class English society. She had no desire to follow in her aunt Adrienne's path, waiting for twenty years for her lover to succeed to his title as Baron de Nexon, and not to be controlled any longer by parental disapproval of the marriage.

A mixture of pride and loneliness gradually led her to reconsider her feelings. The duke's very public pursuit of her began to soften her resistance. After months of persuasion, Bend Or finally secured her agreement to join him on a cruise on his ship, *Flying Cloud*, in the summer of 1924, after the launch of her spring collection. Coco later commented: 'He had a yacht, and that's the best thing for running away to start a love affair. The first time you're clumsy, the second you quarrel a bit, and if it doesn't go well, the third time you can stop at a port.'

They had a wonderful time. The duke finally overcame her resistance on board his four-masted schooner – after all the other guests had departed, leaving behind only a crew of forty and a hidden orchestra. The affair looked promising. Gabrielle was a great sailor, earning the duke's instant admiration, for he had a childish delight in ordering his captain to head directly into the path of any swell, to make his voyages more exciting.

Gabrielle was not so impressed by the sea: the endless empty vistas bored her. But the duke's *Flying Cloud* was luxuriously fitted out, and it was fun to descend on the ports of the south coast, to visit friends, have supper, or go gambling.

Gabrielle had stunned the *beau monde* in Cannes in the summer of 1922 by sporting white slacks and a deep suntan. Previously the south coast had been a wintering resort, patronised by the aged and the sick, particularly from England. Gabrielle launched the fashion for a sunburnt skin, for up until this moment, convention held that a lady always kept a fair skin, a dark one indicating too close ties with labouring peasantry. This was another of Gabrielle's unconscious jeerings at the very society that supported her, by harking back to her humble origins just at a time when the height of social status was tantalisingly available to her. All those weather-beaten, lined faces of women market traders of her own family were not forgotten.

With the duke and Gabrielle constantly present (Gabrielle attired in her latest cruising clothes), the south of France was absolutely confirmed as the place to be. It had been 'discovered' by such visitors as Scott and Zelda Fitzgerald, and gradually, throughout the Twenties, the Riviera became a chic summering resort.

By 1931, the grand hotels were all staying open in the sunlit months, and the crowned heads of Sweden, Norway, Denmark, not to mention the Maharajah of Kapurthala, and stars such as Charlie Chaplin, Maurice Chevalier, Valentino and his wife Alice Terry, were habitués. Various of these celebrities were guests of the duke and Gabrielle Chanel on board his yacht. Meanwhile, the professional hostess, Elsa Maxwell, worked with Prince Pierre, father of Prince Rainier, in staging grand fêtes to draw the jet set to the tiny kingdom of Monaco. Due to her efforts the Summer Sporting Club was opened in Monte Carlo in 1927. She and Gabrielle were, in keeping with all expectations, great social rivals.

Well-planted stories in the British newspapers linked Gabrielle's name with the duke's as his possible future bride. On 13th October 1924 the *Star* reported:

'People are talking a lot about the duke's future . . . Now, people in the know affirm that the new duchess will be a beautiful, brilliant Frenchwoman who presides over the destiny of a great Parisian fashion house.'

All the following summer, Gabrielle and the duke were seen together everywhere. They visited his hunting lodge at Mimizan, where Gabrielle stunned the duke's guests by riding brilliantly, both side-saddle and astride, in immaculately simple outfits. In Paris they visited the opera, and while Gabrielle worked on the costumes for *Le Train Bleu*, the duke often sat in the darkness of the auditorium, causing much gossip as to which of the ballerinas he was considering for conquest.

Coco and the Duke of Westminster
at Eaton Hall, Cheshire

When the duke's estranged wife Violet publicly moved out of his life, Bend Or felt free to ask Gabrielle to visit his English properties. Some of the gaiety of her Royallieu days came back to her then, for there was riding, great cross-country walks, picnics and shoots, in Scotland and in Cheshire. Gabrielle was fearsomely energetic; she ate and drank abstemiously, and charmed all of the house guests by her low-voiced, quick-witted conversation. On one occasion Misia Sert accompanied Gabrielle to the duke's Scottish estate, but felt totally out of place. She asked Gabrielle where the nearest post office was. 'Twenty miles. Can you ride a horse?' Misia was homesick for the urban intimacy of Paris, and later, Coco could be equally dismissive of this period of her life: 'One would do knitting, change clothes several times a day, go and admire the roses in the park, roast oneself in front of a huge open fire in the salon, freeze the moment one moved away from it – that's all a weekend at the stately home consisted of!'

Gabrielle attempted to learn English during this time, engaging the services of a young male secretary to the duke. But she did not make much progress and had even less motivation when the duke forbade her to learn it well, because she would then understand the stupid things he said. Bend Or appealed to Gabrielle because he had an ambiguous sense of self: one moment he would be autocratic, the next positively forlorn – at least in private. Gabrielle had so much strength, and a sense of self, personified as 'Coco', created entirely out of her will to succeed. The Duke of Westminster had in some ways met his match: a woman as commanding as he was himself, and yet as vulnerable as he was, underneath.

Gabrielle was frequently in the company of Vera Bate, who had effected Gabrielle's introduction to the duke. She was the link between Paris and the best of English society (being related on the wrong side of the blanket to the Duke of Windsor, and an intimate of all the aristocratic circles of the country). Gabrielle and Vera were pictured wearing the duke's old jackets over huge men's sweaters, to keep the dew and mist of the heather-covered hillsides from their citified chests. Not very long after, these masculine-cut clothes were to find their way yet again into Chanel's Thirties' collections. Once again, Gabrielle's success came from a pared down, but essentially cross-dressing element in fashion.

The duke's second wife, Violet, finally got her divorce in 1926, and remarried the year after. Once the legalities were over, the gossip about Gabrielle's role as the next duchess began to increase. With his divorce, the duke too began to change his life. He cared less for the formal circles of the British aristocracy, and began mixing with more unconventional types, actors, actresses, sportsmen, rising politicians, writers. Perhaps he too was preparing for a life with Coco Chanel.

But there were serious obstacles to overcome. The most important of these was Gabrielle's dedication to her business. She knew very well that half her attraction in the duke's eyes was exactly her eminence in her chosen *métier*. In some sense she was an unusal choice for Bend Or, having no blue blood, no title, and being almost past the age for child-bearing. On the other hand, her dazzling personality, her fame, her considerable autonomy, fascinated him. He issued her with a chequebook full of signed blanks. Months later Gabrielle returned the book to the duke's secretary, unused. 'I spend my own money,' she declared. The embarrassed young man remonstrated: 'But the duchesses always. . . .' Gabrielle wanted no part of that system of dependence. Coco reflected: 'I could never have given up the House of Chanel. It was my child. I created it starting at nothing.' Bend Or clearly expected himself to be the centre of her life, and that she would, in the end, bend to him.

Iya, Lady Abdy, Gabrielle's close friend, observed the relationship as it intensified: the duke was 'rather a guttersnipe, but Coco liked that. With Westminster Coco behaved like a little girl, timid and docile. She followed him everywhere . . . their love was not sexual.'

It may not have been predominantly physical, but sex certainly mattered, because the duke was determined to produce a male heir to his title and considerable wealth. Gabrielle did not underestimate the importance of this aspect of their relationship and sought medical advice once again. She was now in her mid-forties, and her chances of becoming pregnant were slim. In later years Coco hinted at the 'humiliating acrobatics' which she endured on the advice of various doctors, to ensure that she might conceive. She even suggested that she had undergone surgery in her efforts to satisfy the duke, just as she hinted at something of the sort with Boy Capel, earlier. Coco once said: 'I'm a virgin really, I've never had a child. . . .' In the fundamental part of her nature, this was how she perceived herself: an incomplete woman. It was all without success. She discovered it was too late, and that she was sterile.

Bend Or continued to pay court assiduously, showering her with gifts, including priceless gemstones and a town house in Mayfair. Others of his circle were smitten by Gabrielle's brilliance, and most approved of the unusual match. Winston Churchill, a life-long friend of the duke's, wrote home to his wife from Mimizan in 1927, where he had gone to hunt: 'The famous Coco turned up & I took a gt. fancy to her – a most capable & agreeable woman – much the strongest personality Benny has yet been up against. She hunted vigorously all day, motored to Paris after dinner & is today engaged in passing & improving dresses on endless streams of mannequins. Altogether 200 models have to be settled in almost 3 weeks. Some have to be altered ten times. She does it with her own fingers, pinning, cutting, looping etc. With her – Vera Bate, née Arkwright. "Yr Chief of Staff?" "Non" – "One of yr lieutenants?" "Non. Elle est là, Voila tout . . ."'

The image of Winston Churchill earnestly conversing in half-French, half-English, on the subject of a couturier's life in military terms, is amusing, and says much for Gabrielle's charisma, that she could make her own affairs sound sufficiently grand and serious to put before this British lion.

It was no mere coincidence that in these years between 1924 and 1931, Gabrielle's love of all things English manifested itself in her work. Impudently, a star item of her 1930 winter collection was an evening wrap of ruby velvet with an enormous ermine collar – plagiarised from an English peer's court robes. Copies of the sailors' uniforms from Bend'or's *Flying Cloud* or his other great ship, *Cutty Sark*, formerly a destroyer sent out (with typical British tact) for trade in the Far East, maintained naval precision with double rows of brass buttons and neat standing collars. For the 1930-31 season she had many tweeds specially woven for her in Britain. She developed an unerring ability for recognising whether a fabric really had been made with the water of the Tweed river. 'I only need touch it,' she claimed. In 1932 Messrs Ferguson, textile manufacturers, invited her over to Britain to create designs from their new fabric, cotton piqué – just the loveliest crisp frocks to wear to the races, such as the one worn by Lady Pamela Berry and sketched by Drian. Gabrielle Chanel was one of the top ten Paris fashion designers who regularly advertised their salons in the British press, so close and successful were the links between these two social worlds at the time.

One of her most popular designs was a jersey dress and jacket in a beige and blue abstract design – in spite of her current enthusiasm the eye and taste of the pattern came out of her familiarity with the work of Cocteau, Dali, Picasso. Chanel's individuality remained her strength. This popular design was bought by Jaeger to launch their new fashionable store in Oxford Street.

It was unusual to sell couture clothes in a store – most smart women still went to a dressmaker or couturier. A tiny hint of the revolution in fashion which Chanel would lead in the future. But the advertising – excruciating!

'One of those qualming occasions, my dears – when one has to assemble reserves of intelligence – is choosing the absolute tweed coat. I mean, unless it is perfectly sinless in cut and design nothing can look more bogus. Too completely pseudo – don't you agree?' .

Gabrielle rebelled at the slavish concern with appearance, the whole social preoccupation with looking well-bred, like a lady. She broke the rules at once. She took to wearing drooping English sweaters and jerseys, and piling on them the jewels that the duke gave her – parures that would normally never be seen before six. Misia Sert did the same. Contemptuously, Gabrielle treated gemstones like paste and baubles like gems, often wearing the real and the frankly fake together. Picture one of her star customers, the ballerina Alicia Nikitina, wearing

a severe navy blue Chanel suit as a background to a constellation of immense diamond and ruby bracelets, clips and rings. As Madge Garland, ex-fashion editor of *Vogue* UK describes: 'Chanel's costume jewellery, in reality composed of glass beads from Czechoslovakia, resembled the real stones she loved (and possessed) – huge knobbly emeralds, the pigeon-blood ruby, the dark-as-night sapphire,

Coco in 1929 in her own fashion

great pendants and chains of flashing stones, all the treasures of a rajah's jewel chest, which in simulacre, she now made available to all women.' Except that they were not from an oriental king's caskets, but from a duke's coffers. The notoriety of the relationship added considerably to Chanel's success with this new fashion, to the slightly shocking thrill her clients experienced in emulating her insolent style.

One of Gabrielle's most influential jewellery designers was the Count Etienne de Beaumont. He started designing by making little gifts for his friends, for parties or birthdays. He was very well connected and ran a salon with his wife at his home on the corner of two streets, Duroc and Masseran. He also gave the most extravagant and wonderful parties, usually in fancy-dress, a current craze among the super-rich. He was a great friend of the artist Marie Laurençin and knew all the people one needed to know in Paris. Gabrielle realised that by employing him, all his acquaintances would come to her *maison de couture*; it was another ruse to have the élite at her feet.

This was the age when the little black dress came in – all Gabrielle's doing, for once again the boundaries between the classes were blurred. In 1926 *Vogue* USA had labelled one of her dark little numbers, 'A Ford signed Chanel.' Previously no one had ever worn black – it was exclusively the colour of mourning. Black marocain or crêpe de chine for the cocktail hour, matched with a neat little hat, became the thing – and never mind that the girls serving tea in any hotel or behind any counter in any smart shop, wore exactly the same thing. 'It gave women great delight to play at looking poor without having to be any the less elegant,' the fashion writer Lucien François explained. Gabrielle remembered bitterly a gibe from the society hostess Elsa Maxwell, that as Chanel could not wear mourning for Boy Capel, she had made the whole world wear it. 'What bad taste,' said Coco.

Perhaps Bend Or's lack of snobbery had its subtle influence on Gabrielle's work, besides offering more direct inspirations. Gabrielle wanted the world to be less divided by exterior class symbols. Although seldom directly political, she was an *agent provocateur* in fashion. She took the clothing of the streets and redefined it as the latest thing.

Coco reinvented her past, but occasionally memories were uttered with a spontaneity that verified them, like this wonderful picture of a 'friend' at Eaton Hall:

'Eaton Hall could easily have been disgusting. . . . You see what I mean? If d'Annunzio had lived there, with heaps of dusty tapestries and theatre sets and ridiculous objects, costume ball trinketry. What one had to admire, on the contrary, was the cleanliness of that house, its English unaffectedness. It made one forget the ugly bits. A knight in armour, stuck in the corner of a staircase, that does look a little overdone – unless it has always been there. Then you see it as something that grew out of the earth, proud and straight, especially when the armour is all shiny and looking ready for action. At Eaton Hall there was one in particular, a sort of hidalgo, whose helmet especially – all it needed was a plume – caught your attention. Shut up inside his heap of scrap metal, he became a kind of friend to me. I thought of him as being young and handsome. I said hallo every time I went past. I used to say to myself, "After all, what a clever piece of work that thing is. And how attractive and powerful one must feel inside it." When I was sure no one was looking I used to go up and shake his hand.'

A strange reminiscence, more like a self-exposing reverie that unconsciously releases Gabrielle's desire to be invulnerable and to present a handsome and polished exterior to the world. And the order and cleanliness of Eaton Hall appealed directly to her institutionalised, severe tendencies, dating from her Aubazine convent childhood; the polish, the clear open space of the orphanage. An orphanage and a stately home – for Bend Or with no father, and for Gabrielle with no family ties remaining, these were strange resonances evoking a mutual attraction.

Coco later described the duke as 'the simplest person in the world. With him I saw the acme of riches and rarity. But he did not know the meaning of the word snobbery. It would never have occurred to him. He was simplicity itself, simple as a tramp.' (This was the duke who jumped in muddy puddles when he wore new shoes, to break down the patina of the unused leather!)

There is one anecdote that well portrays their relationship. Once Gabrielle went to the famous hothouses of Eaton Hall and cut all the golden azaleas she could lay her hands on, to complement some crimson curtains. The duke, taking her in to dine, was appalled. 'I wish I knew the swine who did that,' he growled. 'You're arm in arm with him,' Gabrielle teased. 'The only way not to hate azaleas is to cut them.' Bend Or found her irresistible, incorrigible, charming. Gabrielle had a tremendous sense of the comic – it was this quality above all others, that had attracted Etienne Balsan and made him take her to Royallieu as his companion. And, as always, she had an innate gift: she knew how to make a lover feel that he was the first, the only one. The quality of whole-heartedness, sometimes expressed as passion, sometimes expressed in a waif-like hunger for affection, disarmed even an English peer with a limited, or repressed capacity for love.

From Gabrielle's point of view, Bend Or was a soothing antidote to the passion and conflict of her previous love affairs. Going to stay on his various estates was like taking sanctuary, avoiding the pressures of Paris. Coco recalled: 'I'd finally found a shoulder I could lean on, a tree against which I could prop myself. If I

hadn't met Westminster I'd have gone crazy. I had too much emotion, too much excitement. I lived out my novels, but so badly.'

Misia was less romantic. 'When the English are really in love, they give everything. Since the duke treats you like a greedy empress, he must be madly in love with you.'

And Coco, unable to resist a joke at the duke's expense, once quipped: 'Being too rich is as dismal as being too tall. In the first instance, you do not find happiness, in the second, you do not find a bed.'

One is reminded of the marriage of Jacqueline Kennedy and Aristotle Onassis. The Duke of Westminster could certainly buy privacy. He also shared Gabrielle's hearty disregard for material wealth, because he was beyond riches. Gabrielle liked that, coming from the other end of the scale, where material things meant so much that the only defence was to deny the attraction of luxury from the outset. This cultivated detachment was what made wealthy women flock to her side.

For a while, the duke continued to try to encompass Gabrielle's world with his own. He encouraged her to open a boutique in London in 1927, where all the best people came to buy her clothes. With Violet off the scene, Gabrielle slowly began to take up the role of mistress of the house – whichever one they were in – and to receive the duke's guests as his partner, his equal. In 1927, for instance, the duke's daughter Mary had her 'coming out' ball in London, which Clementine Churchill and her daughter Diana attended. Much to the duke's pleasure, Mary invited Gabrielle. In response, Gabrielle gave a pre-ball dinner for Mary and various other friends at her Mayfair house. But at the end of it, she urged her guests to leave, claiming she had to change her dress. When she failed to arrive at the ball, the duke hurried back to escort her. He found Gabrielle in bed, slyly powdered all white, with black make-up smudged round her eyes, claiming to be suddenly taken ill. This was Gabrielle's way of avoiding too head-on a confrontation with Bend Or's formal life: his first wife and numerous other close associates would be at the ball, and she had no intention of presenting herself in an ambiguous role. While many people happily accepted her as the duke's 'consort', there were occasions where her anomalous position was embarrassingly evident.

The Twenties were the age of the 'little black dress' – invented by Chanel

The duke was irritated, then amused by her resourcefulness. He returned to the party – only to find that Gabrielle had made herself the focus of the entire evening, by her absence.

Her independence and decisiveness had its disadvantages. It became clear to the duke that Gabrielle would never leave her work for long. So frustrated was he by her constant trips back to Paris that he had a workroom set up for her at Eaton Hall and brought over her key staff to assist her in the preparation of each new collection. But couture work belongs to Paris, and he could never make her stay away from the capital for very long.

Bend Or's affection continued as strong as ever, but the balance of the relationship was subtly shifting. Gabrielle became more possessive, more desirous of security. In pursuit of him she bought a plot of land, in the south of France, above Roquebrune – La Pausa. It was to be her own place, not a gift from the duke. With her customary generosity she gave a little house on the estate, La Colline, to Vera Bate. A useful gift for this friend who was so well connected with the English first set – and nearby at Golfe Juan, Winston Churchill was a frequent guest at the home of the actress Maxine Elliot. Lords Rothermere and Beaverbrook holidayed nearby at Cap d'Ail. It was the perfect setting for her relationship with Bend Or to flourish, to come to fruition in marriage.

L A   P A U S A

The decision to buy La Pausa came about when she was on the duke's yacht, visiting Monaco. A young architect, Robert Streitz, had seen the plot of land at La Pausa and visualised it as the perfect location for him to build a showpiece villa. A friend introduced him to the Duke of Westminster and Gabrielle at a party on the yacht. The subject of the land came up, catching Gabrielle at a point when she had the same thought in mind, to build a home for herself and the duke. Strangely, Gabrielle referred to the orphanage at Aubazine when discussing her wishes with Streitz. She recalled the central wide sweeping staircase in the main hall at Aubazine, with steps worn down to a curve over the passage of time. 'I visited the place on my holidays. . . . We'll call it the monk's staircase,' she lied, trying to cover the true need in her remark – a barely conscious desire to incorporate her past into her future. Streitz made the effort to go to Aubazine and see for himself. But he found nuns, not monks, and a school for orphans. He remembered meeting the Mother Superior who recalled her now famous charge. Streitz was amazed and curious. The staircase was constructed according to Gabrielle's wishes.

Bettina Ballard, model and former *Vogue* writer, gives a clear picture of La Pausa in her memoir, *In My Fashion*: 'La Pausa was the most comfortable, relaxing place I have ever stayed. It was a complete contrast to the country life that she (Chanel) experienced with the Duke of Westminster. . . . She occupied the upper right-hand wing of the villa with her close friend, Misia Sert. The left-hand wing consisted of a series of suites of two bedrooms and two baths, each joined by their own private foyer. Guests generally arrived in couples married or otherwise, and this gave them complete privacy. . . . The house was blissfully silent in the morning. . . . Lunch was the moment of the day when the guests met in a group, and no one ever missed lunch – it was far too entertaining. The long dining room had a buffet at one end with hot Italian pasta, cold English roast beef, French dishes, a little of everything.'

The house had a simple opulence. The colour scheme as always was brown, beige and white – a specially woven carpet in fawn and brown made the salon comfortable, with divans that could put up unexpected guests. Every room was filled with flowers, among her favourites tuberoses and lavender bunches. Gabrielle's bedroom was more elaborately furnished than her 'cell' at the Ritz, with a huge Spanish gilt iron bed and a view over the garden of olives and cypress trees.

While La Pausa was being completed, Gabrielle tried to deal with another part of her life that might stand in the way of her marriage to the duke. Her two lowly brothers had to be relegated to obscurity. She already supported Alphonse, and had a certain measure of control over him. Since the end of the First World War she had been handing over 3,000 francs per month, a considerable sum for the time. It allowed Alphonse to have a car, something only small-town professionals like the doctor had in those days. He ran a tobacco and drinks store. She simply ordered him to mend his ways, not to get drunk or do anything illegal, and keep to his own patch in the Cévennes where it was unlikely that the connection would be uncovered. Her other brother Lucien was more difficult to deal with as he had some measure of independence and to her great embarrassment calmly continued setting up his stall on market day at Clermont-Ferrand.

She harried him into giving up the life that suited him perfectly well (much against his wife's wishes). Lucien was ordered to find and buy a house in the area, on the vague pretext that Gabrielle herself might choose to retire and live with him, her closest kin. He was always gentler and more compliant than his brother, grateful for the allowance Gabrielle had unfailingly sent to him since 1921. Amazingly, Lucien did as he was told, buying a country house in the hills above Clermont-Ferrand. It was hardly a palace but a charming stone cottage.

Gabrielle was irritated; the house was not grand enough for her story of a country gentleman-brother to look convincing. She refused to consider it as her prospective home. Perhaps then Lucien understood that she would never return, that he was being 'tidied up' by his wealthy, powerful big sister. He would not move again, but he did resign himself to an unemployed life, on his sister's patronage. At least he could remain quietly connected to his old village associates, businessmen, local farmers, and street traders.

Her final effort was to write to Lucien insisting that he cut his ties with the disreputable Alphonse. Lucien, equally amazingly, agreed. Perhaps Gabrielle did not want Alphonse to know how much his brother was getting out of her. Whatever the reasons, this manipulating and obliterating of family ties is a sad reminder of the deep bitterness and resentment that her poverty-stricken past caused her to feel, and sheds an unattractive light on what might at first appear to be shining, sisterly generosity – there was no pure impulse of that sort, only a muddle of motives.

At times Gabrielle could be generous, in a style she learned from the duke himself. On one occasion the photographer Horst did a portrait sitting of her, with which she was well-pleased. He declined any fee from his sitter. In gratitude she invited him to her home. Touring her vast treasury of antiques and *objets d'art*, Horst idly admired a few pieces. Dinner followed, then they left together for a party. But some days after, a van arrived at Horst's home and every piece he had admired that evening was presented to him. This was Gabrielle's fastidious, positively aristocratic way of saying thank you for his flattering work of her.

However, just as Gabrielle's success as a couturier reached new heights, in 1929, she began to hear gossip, that the duke was seeing other women. Their affair had cooled a little, and the duke began to resent the times she preferred her work to spending time with him. There were rumours of his infidelity, and Gabrielle at times threw the most tremendous rages. On one occasion, Bend Or brought aboard a young woman reputedly his latest conquest. Gabrielle was so affronted that she ordered him to dump the young lady unceremoniously ashore at Villefranche. To make amends Bend Or bought Gabrielle a huge emerald from a jeweller's in Nice. He offered it to her, apologising, on the deck of *Flying Cloud*. After considering the opulent object for a few moments, Gabrielle let it slide between her fingers into the sea. Gemstones were the *leitmotif* of this love affair: in a similar row over some other flirtation, Bend Or presented her with a perfect pearl necklace. Imagine Gabrielle's victory as she hurled it overboard into the depths.

Worse was in store. Gabrielle discovered that Bend Or was seeing an English aristocrat; the word was out that the Duke of Westminster had chosen his new wife. Gabrielle's beautiful new home in the south of France was nearing completion, but the love-nest turned into a battleground as Bend Or admitted his infidelity, and took to the Casino at Monte Carlo as an escape from Gabrielle's fury. Gabrielle often rushed back to her work in Paris leaving Bend Or fuming over her threats of launching herself into some other liaison, unable to make the break, drawn back every time she threatened to leave him.

A disaffected group set sail in *Flying Cloud* in August 1929 for a cruise along the Dalmatian coast: Gabrielle, the duke, and Misia Sert whose husband José María Sert was left behind after flaunting his unfaithfulness to her in Paris. José María's new love was a young Georgian-Russian girl, Roussadana Mdivani, very much his junior and given to dramatic bouts of depression when self-destruction seemed the only solution. *Tout Paris* was much diverted by the antics of the Sert household.

At Venice, Gabrielle and Misia went ashore hoping to meet up with Serge Diaghilev. They found him lying desperately ill at the Hotel des Bains, dying of an undiagnosed condition. Parisian doctors had warned him that his diabetes could become fatal. A number of other causes for his decline were suggested by various nervous Venetian doctors, but no one was quite clear how to treat him.

Gabrielle returned to the yacht, but Misia, anxious and sensing that the end was near, refused to leave and stayed on at the Lido in the Hotel Danieli. A night later she received a telephone call from Boris Kochno, informing her that Diaghilev was fading fast. Misia hurried back, and was present early that morning, August 18th, at his death. Misia recalled that Diaghilev's two most loyal collaborators, Serge Lifar and Boris Kochno, immediately fell on each other like savage beasts, rolling on the floor. 'Two mad dogs were fighting over the body of their master.'

There was no money to pay the bills, the doctors, the hotel or the funeral. Misia used up all the money she had and would have pawned her jewels – her most valuable possession being a three-strand diamond necklace, slung on with her day clothes. Misia related what happened in her book, *Misia par Misia*; curiously she never once mentions Gabrielle by name – did Gabrielle herself require the anonymity? '. . . On my way to the jewellers I met a dearly loved friend who, following a presentiment, had hurried to Venice. She had in fact left the town the day before on the yacht of the Duke of Westminster. Diaghilev was already very ill and the boat had hardly reached the open sea when she began to fear the worst and begged the Duke to turn back.'

Gabrielle took responsibility for all the funeral arrangements. The burial was a furtive affair, so as not to alarm hotel guests, *à la Death in Venice* . . .

Very early at dawn three gondolas left the hotel moorings, the funeral cortège. Only four friends attended: Misia, Boris Kochno, Serge Lifar and Gabrielle Chanel, all in white, just as Diaghilev had last seen the women in his hotel room. Delighted, exhausted, he had said: 'They were so young, all in white! They were so white.' (Misia records the wording rather differently as if she were the only woman present at his bedside: 'Promise me you will always wear white . . . I've always preferred you in white. . . .')

Returning to Paris, without Bend Or, Gabrielle resumed her work with fortitude. It was now public knowledge that Bend Or had picked out his third wife. Loelia Ponsonby, daughter of Baron Sysonby. He was, after all, reverting to type. It was simply too humiliating to have come so close to a grand marriage, to have conducted a love affair in a blaze of publicity – and then to be rejected, in favour of an aristocrat. And it was ironic that, at this time, her aunt, Adrienne, finally married her *baron*, Baron de Nexon after twenty years of waiting. Gabrielle had no alternative but to summon great reserves of dignity – to be seen looking invulnerable and glamorous in all her usual haunts, to give the impression that it was her choice that the relationship ended. She told Lady Abdy that she intended to drive Bend Or mad with jealousy by starting up an affair with someone else. The man she chose was her former lover, Pierre Reverdy. When word got back to the duke, he was gratifyingly incensed, and a flow of letters and yet more gemstones revealed his reluctance to let go of his mistress.

Bend Or's biographer, Leslie Field, adds an interesting note to the end of the relationship. 'She never dared say she felt unwell or had a migraine, because he

1931 White Satin

*Coco, Misia and the duke's trip to Venice in 1929 ended sadly
with the death of Diaghilev*

(the duke) would insist on summoning the most famous doctors from Harley Street, and in time she gave up expressing any wishes as they were immediately fulfilled and she was left with none of the excitement of desire.'

The 'excitement of desire. . . .' For a time, Gabrielle had deliberately chosen security, the comfort of riches. But she was by nature combative, and needed the stimulus of challenge. That, above everything else, would have made her break with Bend Or eventually. His essentially empty existence, rushing about from yacht to castle to hunting lodge with no focus for his energies, would have palled. All the same, it was unbelievably insensitive of the duke to push her devotion to the limit, by presenting his future bride to her – to force her to receive Loelia Ponsonby in person as a friend. Loelia described the incident: 'She was wearing a navy blue suit and an immaculate white blouse and lots of necklaces and bracelets. She sat in her great armchair with the coromandel screens as backdrop and she made me sit on a small stool at her feet. I had the impression I was up before a judge, having to decide if I was worthy of becoming the wife of her old admirer. I strongly doubt if I passed the test.'

Cruelly, Loelia recalled later how generous the duke was to her. A small head, neatly curled up hair and a small hat was the current vogue; one day Loelia went to put on her hat and found the dear duke had pinned a fashionable diamond clip to it. He had certainly learnt what was *à la mode*, and how to endear a woman to him. But the jewels, pinned casually to the headgear, were a sign of the times and pure Mademoiselle Chanel.

Gabrielle was now, in the late Twenties, at the height of her influence on fashion, a small comfort in the face of Bend Or's defection. In 1928 she had her salon in the rue Cambon entirely revamped, with floor to ceiling-length mirrors, in the Art Deco mode. Whatever went wrong in her love life, work still remained a stable centre of her existence. Coco: 'When I had to choose between the man I loved and dresses, I always chose the dresses. I have always been stronger than my desires.' In 1929, for example, with the Wall Street crash, several couturiers went out of business, the most notable being Augusta Bernard and Louise Boulanger. Nothing of this economic disaster seems to have affected Chanel. Where other couturiers had relied on the North and South American custom, she was able to withstand the shockwaves of the crash, with scarcely a ripple in the smooth running of her business. In fact the simplicity of her clothes was even more in tune with current feelings. Because the Chanel look was diverse, almost devious, as a fashion, almost anti-fashion in its appeal. Enduring.

At the same time, Gabrielle tried to revive her longstanding relationship with Pierre Reverdy; his five-year retreat to the monastery at Solesmes had been sustainable only while he had faith. Now that faith was weakening. He spent more and more time in Paris, but not comfortably so; every trip only served to remind him of the spiritual peace which he suffered so desperately in losing. He had a hatred for the society that ensnared him, for the world of Grub-Street hack writers, yet at the same time he wanted, more than anything, recognition. That love-hate relationship with the many-headed monster of Society was not unknown to Gabrielle either. That was the source of their mutual attraction. They were both outsiders, using their imaginations to conquer a world that only sparingly offered the reward of esteem. Both determined, perversely, not to value the world's rewards for their talents.

On one occasion there was a revealing exchange of words between Reverdy and Picasso. 'I was made to be a boxer or a toreador,' said Reverdy, referring both to his conflicting attitude to life, and his physique. Picasso, another of life's combatants, replied: 'But poetry, like painting, thank God, is hard work for a man, a violent battle which is played out in one round.'

Reverdy attempted to collaborate with Gabrielle in a volume of writings; she for her part did everything she could to reawaken confidence, faith, some spirit of life and love in a man she valued more deeply than any other lover in her life. Gabrielle's caustic remarks on life are redolent with Reverdy's own attitudes. 'Society is always a bit "high"; you need to pickle it to make it keep. The divine body stinks,' said Coco. 'A woman is a force not properly directed. A man is properly directed. He can find refuge in his work. But work just wipes a woman out. The function of a woman is to be loved.'

This is patently untrue. Gabrielle derived enormous satisfaction from her work – she most certainly was directed in her salon in the rue Cambon. But what she was having to face was that for her success, and the consequent overdevelopment of her ego, a traditional kind of relationship was going to be almost impossible. There are many men who are happy to be passive, or subservient to strong women. The problem was that Gabrielle never found this type attractive.

Gabrielle was convinced that the geographical kinship she had with Pierre Reverdy, their similarity of mentality made them uniquely destined for each other. She thought her vitality would in the end overcome him and win his love. She was a woman of immense will who saw Reverdy's resistance as a challenge, a battle in which she was determined to be the victor.

Poor Gabrielle: no sooner compelled to accept her former lover in public circles, as a civilised friend, and to tolerate the company of his high-born wife; even now her crusade on the rebound to capture this lowly, poverty-stricken, religiously tormented poet began to fail. Why did a woman of such enormous talent and energy fall for such demanding and difficult men?

The answer lies in the apocryphal reply she is supposed to have given the Duke of Westminster on the subject of their marriage. 'There have been several Duchesses of Westminster. There is only one Gabrielle Chanel.' Perhaps the remark gained currency when she knew the liaison was doomed. That these words were soon spread abroad in the world must have given her some solace. But she was only face-saving. It was not an act of defiance. It was a desperate cry for recognition. She had an enormous personality, a demonic capacity for work, and a special, unusual talent that was well-timed and well-placed in a prosperous world. But where was the man who would find in her 'the only one, Gabrielle Chanel'? She hardly ever accepted herself, after such a resounding early abandonment and could never fall in love with anyone who might in all reason give her real affection. She was lost to herself, lost all those years before in the Cévennes, when her father abandoned her to the nuns of the orphanage, and no amount of achievement or acclaim ever truly made up for it. 'Only one Gabrielle Chanel.' It was a challenge to the world but it ought to have been a plea: 'There is only one, isn't there? I am me?'

In bolder mood Coco once said, 'I am no longer what I was. I will remain what I have become . . . I have the dreams of a child. I dream of the life I'd have liked to have.'

Her defence echoes in the words of Pierre Reverdy, in *Le Livre de mon bord*: 'What would become of dreaming if one were happy in reality?'

Reverdy's break with her was not easy. He did not arrive at it without some temporary hostility. He wrote: 'It's time for me to change the way of life to which I have uncourageously abandoned myself for *some ten years* now, if I do not want to end by becoming totally disgusted with myself. . . .'

In other words, he was finally and irrevocably going back to Solesmes. Unfair of him to taint Gabrielle with the sinful aspects of Parisian life! Her love for him was generous and good. She had made every effort to build up his self-esteem, and to help make his words better known. She had financed his work in subtle ways, through his publishers. In the end he knew that she was a fine, remarkable woman, and he remained devoted to her, although only from the distance of a humble cottage, outside the monastery walls.

The hands of Gabrielle Chanel

H O L L Y W O O D

Acknowledging her defeat with Pierre Reverdy, Gabrielle turned once more to Misia Sert for companionship. In the summer of 1930 Misia stayed with her at La Pausa, and the two women were constantly seen together at the smart soirées of the season on the south coast.

They were perfectly attuned to each other's personalities. Misia and Gabrielle were two of the world's greatest gossips. They would sit in a café, or on the sofa at some dazzling party, and comment in minute detail, on the success (or much more frequent) failure of every woman's attire. Every gesture, every glance would be imbued with significance – who was trying to seduce who, which lover was cooling in his ardour. Misia loved drama, and had an unerring tendency to spot emotional crises and to involve herself wherever possible in the final stages of someone's emotional collapse. Gabrielle was more remote, but she loved to hear reports of Misia's adventures. No fool herself, she would wither anyone foolish who tried to ingratiate themselves with her, while Misia, delighted, sat back and watched the final *coup de grace* of a skilled and elegant duellist.

The two women exaggerated a failing they had in common: a tendency to judge the world by its dress, and by its taste in accessories. Still, it must have been fun to be able to condemn utterly some duchess's choice of shoes, and to pass a killing verdict on the cut of some millionaire's cravat. It passed the time, and was essentially harmless.

Misia needed Gabrielle. Her marriage to José María Sert was over, and she had lost the most valued and important relationship of her life. Somewhat bereft, the new role of acolyte in Coco Chanel's life was at least a compensation for her, filling the void with excitement and good company. For Gabrielle certainly attracted the most dazzling characters, and was never short of some thrilling new enterprise.

Imagine the two women's delight, then, when at a party in Monte Carlo, Gabrielle was introduced to none less than Samuel Goldwyn, the head of a major film studio, MGM, and within the space of a few hours, was beguiled into trying her hand as his chief designer – in fact, to dress his stable of stars, on and off the screen. Goldwyn offered Gabrielle an astounding sum of money, a million dollars, a figure she could not refuse. Misia of course was game for the adventure, and so the two women decided to travel to Hollywood together.

In the Thirties, during the Depression, film studios controlled the lives of their 'products', the stars, both on and off the screen. Movie fan magazines were aimed at the more prosperous middle-class females, filled with details of their favourites'

beauty routines and at-home entertaining habits (besides their carefully manipu-lated love-lives). If any actor objected, there were queues of young hopefuls perfectly willing to replace them and submit to the movie moguls. It was an era of escapism, in which film scenarios became increasingly frivolous and the settings deliberately extravagant as a diversion from the harsh realities of life outside the theatre.

Gabrielle's experience of Hollywood was sure to be a mixture of curiosity,

Coco and Salvador Dali at rue Cambon in the 1930s

frustration and amusement. She knew that before she went. She wondered what she would get out of the trip. More business for her salon? But the richest American women came to her already, in Paris. Slightly less rich women bought high quality copies of her clothes in the couture departments of big stores. Simplified versions were sold cheaply through the growing industry of ready-to-wear. It occurred to her that through publicity in film work, she would add more fame and status to her name, not to mention the enhancement of the sales of her perfume, No. 5.

Goldwyn saw in Chanel another way of enlarging his audience. 'Women will go to the cinema for two reasons, one to see the films and the stars, two to see what's the latest thing in fashion.'

The journalist Laura Mount wrote a piece about the new partnership in *Colliers* magazine. 'The idea seems good, even those who are pessimistic recognise that. Mr Goldwyn and Mlle Chanel are sure it's going to work . . .' but she could see the obstacles. 'If Chanel were to create a dress for Bebe Daniels in which the effect depends above everything on its simplicity, Bebe would look at it for a moment and then stick a big rose on it before wearing it. Clara Bow would stick two roses, a paste clip and a bow of velvet knotted like a butterfly and ending with two long streamers! Perhaps not altogether like that but you get the idea. . . . That's why the sceptics persist in having doubts. In the closely-linked worlds of cinema and fashion, it's a good bet that Chanel faces a hard, almost impossible task in Hollywood. . . . How can one single person, even with the genius of Chanel, season after season, be the only one given the task of dressing such a galaxy of stars in all the films carrying the name of Sam Goldwyn and United Artists?'

But the Countess of Forceville, *directrice* of *haute couture* at Bergdorf Goodman in New York, disagreed. . . . 'Only Chanel is capable of doing it . . . Even if they've never wanted to listen to anyone else before, the stars will listen to Chanel. They'll be mad about her creations. Chanel has never been short of imagination. . . . All the fashions which have been the major developments over the past ten or fifteen years have been conceived in her head. This will be a great success and will be a good thing for the cinema.'

Gabrielle thought it was all going to be interesting and amusing – 'to make clothes that will be seen on the screens of every town in every country across the world – it's fantastic, it's exciting! I'll work day and night to succeed at this.'

Elsa Maxwell telephoned the head of Paramount films, Walter Wanger, the day after the news of the Chanel deal came out. 'Should I get Patou for you?' she offered. She got a decidedly negative response.

It was not going to be so easy. First there was the question of temperaments.

Coco in New York on her way to Hollywood, 1931

Here was Chanel, former lover of the ascetic poet Reverdy, caught up in the ludicrous world of Hollywood, where everyone thrived on hyperbole. She liked to say later that her companion in the exploit, Misia, was more affected by the excesses of filmland than she.

The plan was for her to go to Hollywood for several weeks every spring and autumn and dress the likes of Gloria Swanson, Mary Pickford, Ina Claire and Norma Talmadge. It seems impossible that all these individuals would respond with equal enthusiasm to someone imposing a particularly identifiable 'look' on all of them.

Misia and Gabrielle met their friend Maurice Sachs in New York. (He had married an American pastor's daughter during one of his periods of religious fervour.) The studio then supplied a special train for her journey westward, all decked out in white. Gabrielle charmed all the reporters with champagne, caviar, Parisian mannequins and an aura that was entirely French.

When she arrived at the station in Los Angeles, the stars were waiting to receive her. Greta Garbo welcomed her ('Two Queens Meet' said a Hollywood newspaper). Gabrielle was later to dress her to perfection, not in films, but at the time when she retired and wanted to be alone. Gabrielle also met Marlene Dietrich who became a close friend and one of her most loyal clients.

But getting down to work was difficult. Hollywood had its rules, its codes, which limited what she could do. Modesty was the current thing, part of the hypocrisy that limited what could be seen or not seen, done or suggested on the screen, while producing tantalising scenes. 'Total nudity is never authorised,' the handbook stated. 'This rule applies to nudity directly presented as well as in the form of a silhouette, besides any licentious or suggestive element which might be found in other parts of the film. . . .' Love scenes had to be unprovocative; evening dress had to be modestly becoming; and no suggestion of illicit sex was tolerated. A high moral tone controlled everything in Hollywood.

In spite of many restrictions, Gabrielle tried her best to fulfil her task. The London *Sunday Express* reported her progress in February 1932 – how her opinions on what was chic and what was out of fashion, were in the end being overruled. 'Mlle Chanel thinks lounge pajamas are bad taste: no woman would be seen dead in them. And the first film in which the actresses are dressed by Chanel, *Tonight or Never*, what do we see in the first frames? Gloria Swanson in . . . lounge pajamas!'

The scheme did in fact fail. Gabrielle worked on only three films in Hollywood, *Tonight or Never*, *Palmy Days* with Charlotte Greenwood and Eddie Cantor, and *The Greeks Had a Word For it* with Ina Claire.

Fashion designers seldom worked successfully in the cinema. Clothes cannot be the height of fashion, otherwise the image dates too quickly. The best film designers like Adrian had a way of dressing great stars to suit their own character, adapting current lines into something impressionistic, almost symbolic. The clothes become part of the icon, rather than a creative, noteworthy distraction. One thinks of the wardrobes of Joan Crawford, Barbara Stanwyck, Bette Davis, as successes in this respect. On screen, Gabrielle's clothes were tasteful but dowdy. Hollywood is not a place that thrives on understatement. Parisian, elegant simplicity is far removed from what film stars seek to display – and explains why Erté, a designer of fantasies, a decorative illustrator, as well as a costume designer, worked better in Hollywood than the far more distinguished couturier, Chanel. Even he had trouble: Lillian Gish refused to wear the costumes he designed for her. The same happened to Gilbert Clarke, a protégé of Lucile, the London couturier.

Gabrielle liked to say that of all the stars she met only one impressed her, that was Eric von Stroheim. 'Because with him at least there was some justification for the extravagance . . . he was taking a personal revenge. He was a Prussian persecuting Jewish inferiors. . . . At least with him there wasn't any pretence.' How typical of Gabrielle to see to the heart of a performance and define the essential motive. She speaks of von Stroheim with all the aridity of a village gossip. She had a hard, cold eye, and an increasingly harder heart – she was, after all, unloved and approaching fifty.

One of her most enjoyed and memorable nights in America took place in New York where Salvador Dali led her to a night club in Harlem. She saw black musicians 'making love' with their instruments. . . . 'It was a simulacrum of love as the mass is a simulacrum of God. The dances they sweat over now are nothing at all. That was sacred!'

She also went to see the ballet company formed from the remnants of the Ballets Russes, now under the management of Colonel Basil, Leonid Massine and Balanchine. She was accompanied by Misia who was so overcome with nostalgia for Diaghilev and the great days of his Parisian ballet that they had to leave the theatre before the last act.

Comparing England with America Coco said, 'The English hide everything, the Americans show everything! America is dying of comfort! . . . The Americans wanted to tie me down, you see because I out-fashion fashion. But I'm not for sale or hire. In Hollywood the stars are just the producers' servants. . . .'

While in New York Gabrielle spent time researching the American fashion scene, trying to interpret American social mores, their snobberies, their social barriers. She and Misia delighted in the material excess of the place, laughing at one woman who turned her Fifth Avenue apartment into a Spanish patio; or a

Cecil Beaton's portrait of Coco, 1935

Chanel 1934

Vanderbilt who shipped over carved wood panels from a château of the Loire, and had them cut down to size for a new home. Then there was the miracle of Klein's in Union Square, where the cheapest copies of Parisian clothes were chosen in a *mêlée* of bodies in communal changing rooms – ample black girls trying on dresses next to a blonde Polish peasant or a stunningly decked-out chorus girl.

Perhaps the best reward for her efforts was the journey itself. It was Gabrielle's first trip away from Europe, a broadening of her horizons. It reminded her of the huge market for film that existed in America – and if for film, then for other commodities too. Especially her perfumes.

On her way back to Europe, Gabrielle spent some time in England, to restore her sense of values which had been somewhat battered by her experiences in Hollywood and New York. She staged an exhibition of her latest designs in Grosvenor Square, an address lent by the Duke of Westminster. The proceeds went to the War Service Legion, a charity founded in 1918 by Lady Londonderry and Lady Titchfield. The shows attracted five or six hundred people daily for just over a week. All the best names in England came to see her work: Duchesses Sutherland, Beaufort, the Marquess of Cambridge, Ladies Titchfield, Derby, Desborough, and the stage stars Gertrude Lawrence and Iris Tree. Somewhat mollified by this *succès d'estime*, Gabrielle went home to Paris.

The publicity surrounding Gabrielle's Hollywood escapade was not all negative. The name of 'Chanel' had become internationally known, and she found that an honourable defeat was certainly admired more than no attempt at all. Her *maison de couture* steadily expanded in size throughout the 1930s with her increasing fame and prestige. Extra premises in the rue Cambon were acquired – at the peak of her fame Gabrielle occupied four different addresses in the rue Cambon. With the growing popularity of the South of France as a summer watering hole, more and more foreigners, Americans and Latin Americans especially, stopped off in Paris on their way south, and bought whole wardrobes from each new collection. Gabrielle's cruising and beach clothes were particularly admired and, in every collection, stunning black cocktail or evening dresses were eagerly coveted. There seemed to be no limit to the expanding success of her enterprise.

THE
HOTEL RITZ

On her return, Gabrielle met up with an extraordinarily talented man, known to *tout Paris* as 'Iribe'. Paul Iribarnegaray. He came to her salon suggesting that he could design some jewellery for her. The idea of seducing one of Paul Poiret's acolytes, and one of Paris's most successful artistic creators, was irresistibly appealing.

Paul Iribe was Gabrielle's exact contemporary, forty-nine at this time. Originally an illustrator, Iribe had dabbled in magazine journalism from early in the Twenties, forming one of the group who called themselves the 'Beau Brummells', or 'Knights of the Bracelet'. French *Vogue* pictured them: 'A certain dandyism of dress and manner which is a constant characteristic of the group makes them a "school". Their hat brims are a wee bit broader than the modish ones of the day and the hats are worn with a slight tilt, a very slight tilt but enough to give the impression of fastidiousness. Their coats are pinched in a little at the waist, their ties are spotless and their boots immaculate. A bracelet slipping down over a wrist at an unexpected moment betrays a love of luxury.

'The great difference between these Beau Brummells and their ancient name-sake is that, while they are thoroughly imbued with the same love of excellence and luxury, they are also hard and vigorous workers. . . .'

These were the young men who had studied at the Beaux Arts academy (in Iribe's case, architecture), and worked for the famous magazine publisher, Lucien Vogel. His *Gazette du Bon Ton*, founded in 1912, was full of their delightful hand-coloured plates. Others in the group were Georges Barbier, A. E. Marty, Charles Martin, and Georges Lepape. Paul Iribe had founded his own magazine, *Le Témoin* in 1906, which included satirical sketches by 'Jim', none other than Jean Cocteau.

Whereas the other Beau Brummells came from good families and in some cases had private incomes, Iribe was the outsider: no money, and of Basque parentage. It is significant that once again, Gabrielle was falling in love with an 'outsider'. None of her lovers was from the correct, established faubourg society of Paris. Such predictably desirable men bored her. She liked the complexity of men who were unconventional for whatever reason. From the start she allied herself with men who scorned the establishment: Etienne Balsan was wealthy, but cared not a jot for a title or a secure place in the hierarchy. Boy Capel was quite possibly

Jewish in origin, a brilliant man who chose to spend his youth in a world far removed from his final destination: he was a francophile, comfortable in a foreign country, and only in the last years of his life committed to the British ruling class. Pierre Reverdy had no wish at all to belong to any set – even that of his intellectual peers. The Duke of Westminster was something of an anomaly even in his native country: so wealthy and autocratic that he could ignore all the rules with impunity – in other words, not so much an outsider as above any category. Now Gabrielle was exploring the possibility of attachment to a man who had carved out his niche in Paris entirely through the exercise of his native wit and talent – exactly as she had done herself.

Iribe was not conventionally handsome either: 'chubby as a capon' is how Colette described him, with gold-rimmed spectacles, and an ingratiating priest-like demeanour. Iribe had an affected mode of speech too, an assumed air of privilege cultivated by forming friendships with the élite of Paris. He had talent, undoubtedly, but this was overshadowed by the unpleasant air of the sycophant, and a devotion to luxury.

Iribe's most famous piece of work was the delightful set of watercolour illustrations he made for the designer, Paul Poiret – produced as a large volume of plates. *Les Robes de Paul Poiret* was a novel stroke of publicity and was circulated to all the most influential customers in Europe. It remains a collector's piece to this day. But Iribe had that light brilliance of the gifted which made him equally successful designing rugs, furniture, jewellery and textiles. He was the ultimate 'Art Deco' man.

His first marriage was to the actress, Jane Diris. Both she and Iribe managed to augment their at times irregular income through self-advertisement, endorsing all kinds of luxury goods from furs to cars. A second marriage to a wealthy American, Maybelle Hogan, took him to America and to Hollywood where he found a sympathetic patron in Cecil B. de Mille. He designed sets and costumes, including notably *The Ten Commandments*. But he was never popular with the solid ranks of Hollywood designers (over whom he was placed as artistic director for a while). A fiasco on the film *King of Kings* led to his fall from favour. (No doubt he and Gabrielle had many amusing conversations about their mutual difficulties in cinema city.) Iribe was forced to make an ignominious return to Paris, where his wife Maybelle financed the opening of a shop on the faubourg Saint Honoré, specialising in *objets d'art*. Not content with these achievements, Iribe diverted himself with photography and jewellery designing, which is how he met Gabrielle, and how her strange new venture came into being.

Under his influence, Gabrielle kept her activities a closely guarded secret from the public and the press. The apartment in the faubourg Saint Honoré was the setting for Gabrielle's latest experiment – her own jewellery designs. She had the apartment wired for security and bought in a collection of head-and-shoulder waxwork dummies on which to display her fantasies. Gabrielle had been asked to create original pieces by the International Guild of Diamond Merchants – an inspired choice when one recalls that Chanel was at the time famous for popularising fake costume jewellery and disregarding the status of real gemstones. Tecla artificial pearls, on sale in the little boutique near Schiaparelli's shop in the place Vendôme, were considered the ultimate in elegance, preferably looped in several yard-long strands. Yet Gabrielle's latest collection, unveiled in the autumn of 1932, was composed entirely of white diamonds. None of the pieces was for sale, and an entrance fee was charged, to raise money for children's charities – an untypically open gesture from Gabrielle, who was as a rule disdainful of grand society ladies and their publicly charitable good works. As with her funding of Diaghilev's ballet, she normally chose to remain an anonymous benefactor.

Vogue writer Bettina Ballard tells an amusing story about Gabrielle's attitude to priceless gems. 'Returning to Paris on the Train Bleu, Chanel took a series of compartments for her guests (and paid for them too). We crowded into hers for an apéritif before dinner, and I started to sit on a sausage-like suitcase. "My jewels – my jewels – don't sit on them," she cried. Nothing could have looked less like a jewel case. It was an old and bedraggled canvas bag that a man might put his old sweaters and shoes in. She explained she always carried her jewels like this since she had left a conspicuously elegant jewel case in the Monte Carlo station a few years before.

'The station master had instantly recognised her case and taken it himself to the yacht of the Duke of Westminster on which she had been cruising, unaware of the bag's precious contents. The duke, not at all pleased that Gabrielle had left the yacht and him to return to Paris to work, refused to accept the case. He tipped the man generously but told him to keep it until she personally returned to claim it – a very sure way of getting her back to Monte Carlo . . . it cost Gabrielle a huge sum for the man who found the case plus generous *pourboires* to smooth down ruffled feelings in Monte Carlo.

'. . . She opened it that night in the Train Bleu, and to my naïve eyes, it was an Ali Baba scene. The train was hurtling into the night so violently that the jewels jumped on the table – a great jumble of strings and strings of real pearls, necklaces of mixed rubies, emeralds, diamonds and pearls. . . . There was every type and colour of earring. . . . The jewels made us all gay and a little insane in that crowded jewel-box compartment with everyone shouting above the click of the wheels and running their fingers through the stones.'

Gabrielle's attitude towards jewels remained scornful to the last. In a television

Coco back in Paris in the early 1930s photographed by Kollar

interview in 1969, Coco declared: 'I only like artificial jewellery because I think it offensive and undignified to lug about millions of pounds' worth round one's neck, just because one is rich. Jewels aren't made to give people a rich look, they're made to give an air of elegance, or adornment, which isn't the same thing.

'Isn't that like theatre? No, because the point is to make the jewels look as real as possible. You could even mix real and false. We wear fake flowers, why not fake jewels?'

That was the public side of Gabrielle. In private, Gabrielle could act like a female Midas. Serge Lifar described something that he witnessed in 1965: 'One day . . . she opened her jewel boxes for me, and covered herself with gems. She looked like an idol, an icon. There were jewels everywhere, enormous diamonds, gigantic emeralds, pearls . . .'

When the diamond show was opened in 1932, the public was entranced. The jewels were unusual and exquisite – great fan-like collars of necklaces, sparkling yokes to cover the shoulders; bracelets that were cunningly interlocked so that they be worn as one deep wristband or as four smaller items; hair clips and even fringes of diamonds, worthy of a Cleopatra. 'At last,' said the cartoonist Sem, 'look what we've got, the real thing imitating the artificial.'

The high camp splendour of Gabrielle's designs suddenly made clear to her friends the influence at work on her. To the horror of many of her close friends, Gabrielle and Iribe went 'public' and he started living with her. Most of her circle did not think that Iribe was good enough for her – not in the sense of talent, but in his dubious morality and his tendency to control women, while being supported by them. By 1933 his long-suffering wife Maybelle filed for divorce, and in that same year Iribe set himself up anew as editor of his revived journal *Le Témoin*. Following the pattern of his previous marriages, Iribe had persuaded Gabrielle to finance him. She set up a subsidiary company to do just that.

Echoes of other love affairs resounded ominously in this new liaison. Boy Capel had seen the writing on the wall when pre-1919 France became increasingly chauvinistic and anti-semitic in mood. It sent him across the Channel to make a new life. Now nationalism was promulgated again by Paul Iribe, but in a more insidious and nasty form. As always with such extremists, it arose out of his insecurity as an outsider in his adopted Parisian circles. The enemies of France were Jewish or communistic on the one hand, or the uncivilised democratic mediocrities of America. In fact, everyone not pure French was an enemy. Just as Pierre Reverdy left his mark on Gabrielle with his cold, stoical views of art and faith, so now Paul Iribe infected Gabrielle Chanel for the first time with a political view that was as far to the right as it was possible to be. Whether Gabrielle wished to share these views with the public or not, she was forced into admitting them

by default, because Paul Iribe used her as a model for his portrait of 'Marianne', the symbol of the French Republic. His likeness of her appeared on the cover of his magazine, in every edition.

Le Témoin had a limited readership but enough to form part of the groundswell that resulted in the Fascist riot of February 1934. Forty-thousand demonstrators thronged the place de la Concorde and proceeded from there down the Champs Elysées to the presidential palace. The uprising was aborted in the early hours of the following day.

Gabrielle began to rely on Iribe, drawing him into her organisation as her right-hand man. He represented her at extremely delicate meetings with the board of Les Parfums Chanel where he discussed the rights and wrongs of her numerous lawsuits against the Wertheimers. Ever since her initial agreement with the Bourjois company had come into being, Gabrielle had claimed that she had been gypped by the Wertheimers. She used every legal and illegal trick in the book to wrest back power, or at least, to cause her partners maximum damage. Up to the outbreak of war, there were four court cases.

The board were justifiably offended by this complete stranger walking into their meetings and purporting to represent Mlle Chanel's wishes. The Wertheimers made it clear they would not accept proposals or negotiate new terms with a mere delegate. Gabrielle was furious.

Coco with Fulco de Verdura, a Sicilian duke and jewellery designer,
whose jewellery was to become part of her repertoire

Her friends worried. It became clear that Iribe was beginning to exercise considerable influence in her professional as well as her private life. The most loyal friends thought it was undue influence, and disliked him for it. Once again there were stories circulated of an impending marriage. Gabrielle, getting married at last? Some did not think so. Serge Lifar was sure that the relationship would end badly. 'He dominated her and she could not stand that. Soon she came to hate him as much as she had loved him.'

Gabrielle, getting married? She was fifty years old and making a serious bid for a permanent relationship. So promising did she view this chance for domestic happiness that she cut many ties with her former life, as if anxious not to discourage Iribe by too great a show of independence. She sacked her household staff, including the ever-faithful Joseph, and gave up her apartment on the faubourg Saint Honoré. She moved with only a personal maid into a suite at the Ritz, just across the road from her rue Cambon house. Its front exit faced directly on to the place Vendôme, site of her new arch-rival's boutique: Elsa Schiaparelli. All this was done in unconscious preparation for the new life she would lead as Paul Iribe's wife.

Simultaneously he was changing his ways too. Maybelle now had a judicial separation from her husband, who in turn moved into Gabrielle's summer residence on the south coast, La Pausa. Here Gabrielle and Paul played at their roles of husband and wife, and once again she gave the impression that she actually liked to be dominated. No one will ever know if this relationship would have become irksome to her. Women in love can build fantasies of their true natures, as if casting aside their qualities, their strengths, in exchange for love and security, will bring them happiness. Would Gabrielle eventually have reverted to type? In her relationship with the Duke of Westminster, a similar attempt at docility did not last, and caused the end of the affair. Perhaps not: perhaps now she was feeling old and tired, in need of companionship, and willing to try harder to make a marriage work.

There were threatening developments on the political scene which could have influenced her wishful thinking, and made her anxious for stability. Germany was re-arming, and the Saar was re-annexed to that country. The Nazi party was gaining supremacy, and many people were saying that only a war would resolve the tensions of Europe.

For a while Gabrielle immersed herself in work, producing stunning collections of neat little day suits and extravagant costumes for evening wear – boas of black coq's feathers over a white organdie dress was a particular success. After launching the spring collection for 1935 she went back to La Pausa for a second summer with Iribe.

Coco wearing the costume jewellery she made famous, in the 1930s

Coco at a ball given by Comte Etienne de Beaumont in 1935

Then it all went wrong. One day she walked down from the villa to her tennis court, to join Iribe for a game. She called out to him not to hit the ball so hard (being Basque he played in the style of *pelota*). He took off his sunglasses to say something to her, then collapsed at her feet. He had suffered a heart attack, was rushed to hospital in Menton, but did not regain consciousness. That was the end of Gabrielle's hopes of happiness.

Paul Iribe may not have been a wise or good man, but in other particular ways he was a match for her. He understood ambition, he recognised her great talent, and he was prepared to be at her side. It was a terrible blow and Gabrielle never fully recovered from it. Coco: 'Lovers! I'd say to women, jump out of the window if you're the object of passion. Run from it, if you sense it. Don't dream about grand passion. It's not love. Love is warmth, tenderness, affection, decency. There are so many ways to love and be loved. Remember this though: passion always goes, and boredom stays.'

'Boredom' was to be an important word in Gabrielle's vocabulary from now on. Naturally, friends tried the same old remedies of companionship and work. Misia Sert offered herself as confidante and Jean Cocteau began speaking of a new venture, a play she could dress, called *Oedipe Roi*.

Truly, her professional life was an outstanding achievement. By 1935 Gabrielle employed more than 4,000 people and sold 28,000 dresses in Europe, the Middle East and America. She cannot be criticised for self-pity with the words: 'I remember only that I've been miserable in a life that from the outside seemed magnificent.' The truth of that is undeniable, but the cause lay as much in herself as in the tricks that fate played on her. She was too independent for any man, however gently she tried to express her feeling: 'I never wanted to weigh more than the weight of a bird on any man.' A suitable image: birds take flight, it is their nature never to rest for too long.

By spring 1936, the social unrest in France began to boil over into the streets. Anti-semitism was rife among the conservative elements, while on the left, workers grew militant in opposition. The German army was massing on the banks of the Rhine but the English and French powers tried not to see the significance of what was happening. Ethiopia had been invaded by the Italian Fascists in 1935, with massacres of the populace. The League of Nations voted to apply economic sanctions to Italy, thus heating up the political temperature in Europe.

For a while a sharp sense of futility hovered in the air. Escapist films, such as the Astaire-Rogers dancing extravaganzas, or the exotic decadence of Marlene Dietrich's *Blue Angel* and *The Garden of Allah*, were intensely popular. Greta Garbo proved sensational in stylised romances, like *Camille*. Gabrielle diverted herself too, attending Comte Etienne de Beaumont's masked balls – the economic depression seemed to have left the French élite unscathed. The influence of the cinema could be seen in many of the couturier's slithery, romantic evening gowns: monochrome, black or white fabrics, with a surface sheen or an interesting texture, satin, lace, fur, sequins, net – these were the substances of escapist fantasies. Illustration of fashion moved more into the hands of wonderful new photographers, Horst, Beaton, Baron Hoyningen-Huene, replacing artwork illustrations. These men filled the pages of *Vogue* with their atmospheric portraits of society belles done up to the nines.

Gabrielle's clients, however, were shocked into reality. They finally had to face the collapse of their complacent superiority with the voting into power, in April 1936, of the left-wing Front Populaire. By May France was on the brink of a crisis, with workers occupying factories and national shut-down looming.

Reminding herself of Iribe's form of patriotism, Gabrielle condemned the strikers as lunatics. The facts that many workers were grossly underpaid, and that the right to form a trade union did not exist in France at this time, were completely irrelevant to her. The strike rapidly spread from the male strongholds (railways, car plants, steel and mining industries) to affect her directly through the downing of tools of the textile workers. This increased her instransigence. To Gabrielle there were no rights or justifications on the side of the strikers. They were fools who should come to their senses. '. . . You think all that was about wages? Well, I can tell you the contrary. . . . People caught that thing like the plague, like Spanish 'flu, like sheep catch the staggers. . . .' Typical of her to find a country image for the betrayers, and to demean the intelligence of the nation's workforce.

Eventually, the unthinkable occurred. The girls of the Chanel *maison de couture* occupied the premises. A delegation went to the Hôtel Ritz to present their new terms of work to their proprietor, but Gabrielle refused to acknowledge their existence and sent down a dismissive message that she was still in bed. Then, the final act of treachery took place. She went down the rue Cambon to her own front door and was refused entrance.

Negotiations were protracted and difficult. At first Gabrielle refused to consider any of her workers' demands, even for commonplace rights covering hours, holiday pay and contracts of employment. Her counter-offer, to hand over the whole business to the workforce – provided she alone ran it – was seen as a specious attempt to maintain her singular grasp of her affairs. In the end, with her autumn collection in jeopardy because of the work stoppage, she had to give in to the girls' demands.

Coming so soon after Iribe's death, this strike was the final nail in the coffin of her optimism. Her staff had betrayed her – life itself had cheated her of happiness

The bespectacled Paul Iribe, whom Coco hoped to marry, outside her villa La Pausa

and security. The worms of bitterness and gall fed on the corpse of her goodwill. Gabrielle was a changed personality.

For a while she stood her ground with determination. In 1937 the Exposition des Arts et Techniques was opened in Paris, and Gabrielle made several regal appearances, exquisitely dressed and looking less than forty, not the wrong side of fifty. She spent the summer at La Pausa and the following autumn was back at work, launching the new short-length 'dinner dress' in black organza. Her arch-rival Schiaparelli scored a worrying success with her own version, ballet-length, with high-heeled shoes and flirtatious lacings up the leg, like a tango dancer's.

'That Italian artist who makes clothes' is how Coco described Schiaparelli. Her rival was from a good Italian family; her background was the antithesis of Gabrielle's. 'Scap' wrote poetry, studied philosophy and could hold her ground with anyone in Paris in terms of intellectual opinion. Her lover was Louis Aragon, a poet and a leading figure of both Surrealist and communist circles. Whereas Iribe had idolised everything luxurious and regally French, Aragon delivered parcels for his mistress, who poked fun at the establishment. In 1928 Schiaparelli opened a shop called 'Pour le Sport', and a year later enlarged her business by opening a couture salon. She commissioned Dali, Bérard and Cocteau to design her textiles and other accessories, such as mad little buttons in the shape of hands or butterflies. Her hats were infamous: shaped like an upturned shoe or a lamb chop plonked on a felt plate. If Chanel's quiet good taste epitomises the look of the 1920s, then Schiaparelli's joky clothes do the same for the 1930s. (A modern-day equivalent subversive talent might be seen in Vivienne Westwood.) She was particularly popular in the USA. Her clothes were entirely different in appeal from Chanel's. Schiaparelli brought surreal touches to her designs, such as pockets embroidered to look like a pair of red lips; a fabric printed with tears on it, like a ripped canvas; giant zips which had all the oddity of a Dali painting; padlocks and chains in place of other fastenings; and a wonderful sense of colour (she invented a hot pink, called 'Shocking' and named her own perfume after it). In 1935 she moved into premises in the place Vendôme, opening the first couture boutique, selling limited editions of ready-to-wear clothes, mostly sweaters, blouses, scarves and jewellery. There was a deep and mutual antagonism between her and Chanel, not the least caused by Schiaparelli's confident, well-born manners and of course, her success.

1938 marked the year that *tout Paris* dressed with Schiaparelli, possibly adding weight to Gabrielle's growing disenchantment, her doubts about continuing her couture business, although she always maintained an air of scornful ignorance about anyone else's work. Balenciaga said of them both: 'Coco had little taste but it was good taste. Schiap had lots but it was bad taste.'

But the main reason for Gabrielle's gloom was this battle with her workforce. Just as she had considered herself betrayed by her father, so now she was publicly betrayed by her own staff. She never really forgave her employees, and a certain degree of paranoia crept into her comments on their work from this time forward. Gabrielle believed in the old-fashioned system; she was an autocrat who expected unswerving allegiance and obedience from her staff. This was a peasant attitude; the only change was that she had become one of the bosses instead of remaining in the subservient class.

Coco always complained that her staff did not satisfy her. 'Do they want to become tramps then? They haven't even a tradesman's sense of honour. They don't realise they're working for their own good, to provide for the winter.' Echoes of her peasant past can be heard, when families harvested the chestnuts in the Cévennes, working non-stop when the crop was ripe, and laying up money for the lean, empty months.

Gabrielle was not asking more of her staff than she demanded of herself, which was a total dedication to the work in progress. She thought nothing of working all day and all night if needs be, and expected everyone to understand the urgency of the moment. The novelist Colette draws a word-portrait of Chanel in *Prisons et Paradis*, which conveys the compulsive nature of the latter's working method:

'Chanel works with ten fingers, with her nails, the side of her hand, with her

Coco playing the accordion

palms, pins and scissors, right on the garment, a misty white thing with long pleats, spattered with crystal drops. Sometimes she falls to her knees in front of her work and grasps it firmly, not to worship it, but to punish it a little more, to tighten the cloud of fabric across the thighs of her angel-model, smooth away a little fullness in the tulle. She shows the fierce humility of a person engaged in their favourite task. . . .

'She speaks as she works, in a low voice, deliberately restrained. She talks, she teaches and criticises everything with a kind of exasperated patience. I can make out repeated words, crooned like the most essential musical themes: "How I hate these little puckers! How many times do I have to say, again and again, that fullness is slimming. I won't repeat myself again – press down here, give a little ease there, let's have no little fripperies stuck on a fabric which needs nothing besides its self to look perfect. Smooth it out here, let it out there, no, don't make it too tight . . . I'll never stop saying. . . ."

'She closes her eyes with a distinctively feminine gesture, and presses a fabric close to her cheek, an antelope, sheared fur with its wild, strong odour, and I suggest in a murmur, how perfect it would be for a long slow walk in winter and dozes in a car, all under this antelope coat. With my eyes closed, I can suddenly see those dark pupils, dark like sparkling granite, the colour of mountain water pooled in a hollow of a sun-warmed rock, and Mademoiselle Chanel swiftly rejects my image of fur-muffled laziness.

'"That? It's meant to be worn for hunting wild boar."'

(Something she had done with the Duke of Westminster, at his French estate at Mimizan.) Colette's portrait was published in 1935, but that sure touch she describes began to fail Gabrielle in the late years of the 1930s, leading up to the Second World War. Her costumes for *Oedipe Roi* by Cocteau in 1937 were nothing short of disastrous, which the press did not hesitate to make plain. They made the actors 'look like victims from a casualty list or diapered infants, depending on whether they were tall and pale or pink and podgy', records Edmonde Charles-Roux.

With the German invasion of part of Czechoslovakia in September 1938, Gabrielle's loss of confidence was mirrored in the collapse of the old order. She carried on her glittering life, being seen, indispensable at gala evenings – such as the opening night of the Ballets de Monte Carlo, a company that took over many of Diaghilev's former stars.

She made an immaculate spring collection in 1940, showing one of her prettiest suits, black velvet with a triple frill round the neck, a model that Madge Garland (ex-fashion editor of *Vogue* UK) considered inspired by Watteau. But wasn't black

Coco at a masked ball in 1937

with a white collar yet another revival of the colours of childhood, the nuns, the schoolgirls, the uniforms of her misery?

Finally, Gabrielle opted out. In spite of great criticism from the couture establishment, with the Occupation she closed the doors of her salon. The members of the Chambre Syndicale de la Maison de Couture considered it their patriotic duty to protect the supremacy of the French industry, and to resist any plans the Germans had of relocating the entire edifice in Berlin. Lucien Lelong had been elected Chairman of the Chambre Syndicale in 1937, and had to negotiate with the German authorities when France was occupied. In 1940 he travelled to Berlin to plead his case: Paris had to remain the capital of couture because of the age-old subsidiary industries centred in the city, serving the designers' houses. Nowhere else in Europe had such a complex of varied skills, with button-makers, embroiderers, trimming makers, pattern cutters, and all the other specialist activities. Lelong reopened his salon in 1941, and helped to keep the industry alive. Schiaparelli did her duty too, travelling around America giving lectures on fashion, keeping the name of chic Paris in everyone's mind.

Even in war time, there were customers: wives of German officers, and the 'BOF' women (*beurre, oeufs et fromage*: butter, eggs and cheese), the wives or girlfriends of the war profiteers. Many of the designs produced during the

Chanel with the painter and stage designer, Christian Bérard, at a supper to celebrate the opening of the Ballets de Monte-Carlo in 1938

Occupation were peculiarly heavy and almost distorted in their vulgarity. There were subtle ways of making a gesture of defiance.

But Gabrielle would have no part of this subtlety. At first she went to live with her protégé, her nephew André Pallasse. He took Gabrielle and his family to stay at a hotel in the Basses Pyrénées. Gabrielle had bought the Château de Lambeyc, near Pau, as a home for André, but sitting out the war in such rural isolation began to pall.

The rest of her family would not be countenanced either. She had already pushed Alphonse and Lucien into relative obscurity during her liaison with the Duke of Westminster. Now, summarily, she informed both her brothers that she was discontinuing her allowances to them. She claimed it was a question of money, but with the continuing success of Chanel No. 5, this was a lie. Alphonse took the news with typical sangfroid; Lucien, always more soft-hearted, was badly hit and regretted having given up his market business. Yet even in despondency he had the kindness to offer his sister a helping hand financially. Unmoved by his concern, Gabrielle persisted in her plan to cut herself off, and saw neither of her brothers again. Nor did she acknowledge or aid any of her brothers' families for the rest of her life. Her past became definitively a closed chapter. In fact she had torn the pages from the volume. Later Coco explained that she had gathered up all documentations of her past in order to be able to apply for visas, or other legal requirements of the Occupation. A convenient cover story at a time when bitterness and egotism, never very far from the surface, etched themselves deeper in her personality.

In 1940 she returned to Paris from the south, as did many Parisians after the initial shock of the German Occupation which had led to *l'Exode*. A compelling reason for her return was that her nephew had been arrested. She wanted to do whatever she could to secure his release, most particularly because he had very poor health.

The Ritz was full of Nazis. Her apartment there had been stripped of its contents. Gabrielle was unimpressed by the proximity of the enemy and insisted on having a small room in the hotel for sleeping; for the daytime she would arrange a room above her salon in the rue Cambon. 'What's the use of changing?' she shrugged when friends protested. 'Sooner or later all the hotels will be occupied. Then what? I may as well stay here. My room is too small? Then it will be cheaper.' This was the indomitable Coco who had been through a war before. But it was also the sangfroid of a Parisienne with a German lover.

Chanel: 1938 White Satin and Lace

Chanel 1939: Tricolor number – the last evening dress presented by Chanel before the declaration of war

Gabrielle would never reveal how or when she met her Nazi officer. She claimed to have known him for years. And he had certainly been visiting Paris since 1928. The Baron von Dinklage was known by the nickname 'Spatz' (sparrow in German), and was born of a minor Hanoverian nobleman and an English mother. He was tall, blond, charming and intelligent, an officer of one of Königs Ulanen regiments that served on the Russian front in 1914. His marriage to a girl of good family ended summarily in 1935 when he discovered she had Jewish ancestry. When he met Gabrielle he was in his prime: forty-three years old. Gabrielle was fifty-six, although she could pass as his contemporary with ease.

Years before the war, Spatz was involved in the Nazi cause. His fluent French and English (Gabrielle said they always spoke English to one another) and his easy sociability made him a prime candidate for the job. The only record of his activities confirms that in 1933 he worked for the Reich Ministry of Propaganda; after that his activities remain a mystery but all signs point to espionage. Not a trace of his subsequent career is to be found in any official documents.

Spatz had already had a French mistress before Gabrielle, a woman of good family who, on his account, was accused of collaborating with the enemy. She was imprisoned by the French in the unoccupied zone until the Germans gained sway there too and allowed her to go free. (Not before Spatz had presented himself at her mother's house and offered to secure his former mistress's release in return for active collaboration of the kind her daughter had never been involved in.)

Gabrielle must have known of his past. Did her legitimate cause, to secure the release of her nephew André, persuade her to ignore the truth of his character? His continuing presence in France perhaps led her to think that he was less fanatical about Germany's supremacy than he was about amusing himself and keeping out of trouble. Incredibly, she criticised him for his lack of fervour. What a strange complaint from a French woman in occupied Paris.

Gabrielle and Spatz lived through the Occupation in relative seclusion at the Ritz. Occasionally she went out, to *vernissages*, or to see the ballet at the Opéra, under the direction of an old close friend, Serge Lifar.

Such collaboration was reprehensible, of course. Even more disgraceful was Gabrielle's use of the Occupation to try to regain control of her perfume company. She had long been in partnership with the Wertheimers, and now under new Nazi rulings had a foolproof excuse to rid herself of these men, who manufactured and handled her perfume sales. The basis of her attack was that they were Jews and she was Aryan. Not only that, but she was an 'Auvergnate' like her friend

Laval, arch-traitor and head of the Vichy Government. (She had never ever claimed this origin with pride before.) She also had the backing of Spatz and influential German authorities in her favour.

But the Wertheimers were too clever for her, and too well protected by French people who did what they could to help Jews maintain their rightful possessions. Pierre and Paul Wertheimer sold their property in France to an 'aeroplane manufacturer' for a nominal figure, $2,500, and he, being Aryan, could legally be the new proprietor.

Gabrielle had boycotted the executive board of the company since the days when Paul Iribe had been refused powers as her substitute at their meetings. She tried now to put in her own appointee, a man called Georges Madoux, who had no qualifications for the job. Then a cousin of the Wertheimers, Raymond Bollack, found a German willing to front the company and they made up false transfers of powers that were backdated, so that the purchase by the 'aeroplane manufacturer' was impeccably legal.

However, there may have been some genuinely sore feelings on Gabrielle's part that excuse her behaviour in a small degree. The Wertheimers knew before the war what they were going to do: they stockpiled supplies for shipment out to the USA well before the Occupation of France. Even key personnel were sent to America when the time finally came to flee France. They opened a small factory in Hoboken, New Jersey where they manufactured Chanel No. 5, not to exactly the same specifications as in Paris, because supplies from Grasse were difficult to get. The US company, Chanel Inc, was an entirely separate body from the French company, and so Gabrielle's royalties were reduced to a negligible amount. The Wertheimers secured their lead in the field in the USA by launching an enormous advertising campaign – spending far more than Gabrielle's original investment in the company. Soon Chanel No. 5 was being sold through all the American military PXs.

Even more galling, from Gabrielle's viewpoint, was that the Frenchman put on the board by the Wertheimers was Robert de Nexon, the half-brother of her aunt Adrienne's husband Baron de Nexon: a man who must have been told stories of her Moulins days, when she hoped to conquer the world by becoming a *chanteuse*, and had displayed herself in a *café beuglant*. This was familiarity of a sort that infuriated her, and probably added asperity to her dealings.

Defeated in her commercial forays, Gabrielle conceived of a plan that was as daring as it was ludicrous. There can be no other explanation but that it sprang from *folie de grandeur*. While the majority of the allies wanted to fight the war to the bitter end, and exact the ultimate penalties from the aggressors, a small minority in both France and England wanted a negotiated peace, in order to avoid more bombing of civilians. The majority stood behind Roosevelt and Churchill's decision, taken at Casablanca in 1943: unconditional surrender, no less was acceptable. Negotiation might leave the Nazis with territories they would never surrender.

The Duke of Westminster, however, was for a negotiated peace. There is no evidence to prove that he and Gabrielle were in contact but, in the light of Gabrielle's newest scheme, it seems plausible. She formed the intention of pleading with Churchill directly, in person, to reconsider his view and to throw his effort behind those who wanted a negotiated peace.

The opinion of a close friend of Gabrielle's, Maurice Sachs, is worth considering here. He believed that Gabrielle had developed a certain confidence in her ability to achieve anything she chose to do, not only from her own resources, but from constant contact with men who 'had the certainty that they were going to leave their mark in the world by their works. She had learnt the language spoken by the immortals of the world. This was not disgraceful, because she did so with good grace. . . . She was surrounded by illustrious men. These friendships marked her life. They gave her a grandeur. But she had to be ready to accept it.' When world events had been casually discussed in her hearing by the pride of European lions, politicians and intellectuals, Gabrielle's presumption looks a little less preposterous.

Spatz introduced Gabrielle to an old friend who made her wild notion seem more feasible. Rittmeister Theodor Momm was a cavalry officer from a family who had made their fortune in the textile industry. He was born and raised in Belgium. He thus had two attributes that endeared him to Gabrielle: he understood her world of couture and he was a champion rider – the kind of man she could trust. He also procured the release of her nephew André, and for this she was indebted to him; he succeeded where Spatz had failed.

It was to Theodor Momm that she confided her plan of wooing Churchill. In later years Momm confessed that it was the force of her unique personality that persuaded him there was a chance of her audacious plan succeeding. Gabrielle convinced him that her intimate knowledge of the English mentality, her charm, and her powerful belief in her cause would carry the day.

Momm journeyed to Berlin to take preliminary soundings of the Nazi hierarchy. Gabrielle's intention was to head for Madrid to make contact with Sir Samuel Hoare, the British Ambassador, with whom she was already well acquainted. Hoare would act as go-between with Churchill. A pass for her to travel out of France was her first requirement.

The Ministry of Foreign Affairs would not countenance the scheme. In the end, Momm took it to the Reich Central Security Office, the SS headquarters under

the control of Himmler. AMT VI, the branch dealing with foreign intelligence, was the arm of the vast SS edifice that finally listened to him.

Walter Schellenberg, the head of AMT VI, had a distinguished record as one of Hitler's best spies. He was the archetypal Nazi: blond, handsome, intelligent, ruthless – and barely thirty years old, one of the youngest stars of the Reich. In finding his way through the labyrinth of the Nazi intelligence service to Schellenberg, Momm was doubly lucky. Schellenberg had imagination, and was one of the few high-ranking officers who privately held the view that a negotiated peace with the Allies was the best way to end the war in the west, so that the Reich could continue its advances in the east.

Schellenberg indicated that a pass from France to Madrid would be issued from his Parisian headquarters. Gabrielle was to make her journey in absolute secrecy, and the code name for her expedition was to be 'Modelhut': Operation Hat – a fitting irony for a couturier who had started her career in millinery.

Perhaps Schellenberg was persuaded to let the mad scheme go forward because he had such a tight and professional espionage structure already in place in Madrid – a city he had visited many times in his spying career. There were good men to keep an eye on Gabrielle and ensure that her activities were such as she claimed them to be. Perfectly placed was Prince Hohenloe, member of Madrid's high society and a proven servant of Nazi intelligence. Gabrielle could not put a foot wrong without Schellenberg discovering her duplicity immediately.

Gabrielle, however, was not in the least impressed or intimidated by the orders resulting from Momm's Berlin trip. She was to start out at once and to travel alone – two orders she flatly refused to obey. With all the irony of the best spy fiction tales, she declared that she never went anywhere alone and needed to take a valued companion. She wanted Vera Bate: the woman who had introduced her to the Duke of Westminster, who knew the British aristocracy intimately, and who was on familiar terms with Winston Churchill.

Despairing of her obstinacy, Momm was forced to go back to Berlin and reiterate Gabrielle's terms. She would go with Vera Bate or not at all. What neither he nor Schellenberg knew was that Gabrielle had already taken action to secure Vera's 'co-operation'.

Vera Bate was living in Rome with her Italian husband, and had not seen or had other contact with Gabrielle for four years. Imagine her surprise when a German officer brought her Gabrielle's letter, urging her to come to Paris. The supposed motive was for Vera to assist in the reopening of the *maison de couture*. 'Do exactly as the bearer of this message tells you,' said Gabrielle, evidently beginning to enjoy her role at the centre of a political intrigue.

But Vera refused to go. Her husband was fighting with the partisans, hiding out in the Frascati Hills. She wanted to be near at hand to receive news of him. Within two weeks of her refusal, Vera Bate was taken prisoner and held in the women's gaol in Rome.

Perhaps it was Spatz who ordered the arrest. Perhaps he was the officer who delivered the letter. No one knows for certain except that this action caused a rupture in his relationship with Gabrielle. From now on she had allegiance only to Momm and Schellenberg on the 'Modelhut' plan.

In Berlin, Schellenberg was in no mood to hear of Gabrielle's new demands or of the tactless behaviour of agents from another department in Rome. By the end of 1943 the Nazi hierarchy was riven with factions, demoralisation, plot and counter-plots. He had no time for espionage plans that did not progress smoothly or yield immediate results. The Gestapo in Rome defended their actions by suggesting that Vera Bate was suspected of being a spy for the Allies.

Such was the state of deluded power in Schellenberg that this admission delighted him. If Gabrielle's 'chaperone' was an agent, then what better companion could there be for the expedition. It increased his control over Vera: the fear of death would make her accept his orders.

So two SS officers were delegated the task of escorting Vera Bate from Rome to Paris – a journey on which she was to be treated with all due deference. With some of the pomp and nonsense of a 'B' movie melodrama, Vera was taken from prison to her home to pack up a few belongings and thence to Milan, in the company of a dear old friend (a German aristocrat in the service of the SS, Prince Bismarck), and the SS escorts.

Vera refused once more to leave Rome until it was put to her that she had only two choices, Paris or prison. The following day she accepted Gabrielle's supposed offer and set out with the Prince, the SS officers and her enormous pet dog, Taege. It had been arranged for her to stay in Milan with one Count Borromeo in the splendid castle of Arcore. Theodor Momm met her there to take her on the last lap of the journey to Paris. As this entailed travelling in a small light aircraft, Vera had to leave her precious Taege in the care of a bemused Prince Bismarck and to fly alone with Momm and the pilot.

The drama did not end there. Bad weather forced the plane down at Ulm and the rest of the journey was made by train. By now Vera was convinced that something more than the revival of a couture house was in the offing. Her suspicions were not allayed by her first meeting with Gabrielle at the Hôtel Ritz. Here it was revealed that the new salon was to open in Madrid, not Paris.

Vera allowed herself to believe in the scheme if only out of longstanding affection for a woman who had been a loyal friend for many years. But by the time they reached Madrid, both women had, unknown to one another, formed separate plans – each wanted for different reasons, to secure an audience with the British Ambassador. Vera's aim was to join forces with the British in Italy and get back to her husband as the Allies advanced.

Madrid was seething with refugees. The Hotel Ritz, where the women stayed, was the setting for an elaborately choreographed dance of the spies. English, French, Spanish and German officials in mufti, watched each other and noted any arrivals or departures. Gabrielle set about her mission, cooking up excuses to go out alone and to keep Vera, her trump card, in their hotel suite. In the end the inevitable occurred: the women came face to face with each other at the British Embassy.

Gabrielle had no choice but to reveal her scheme to Vera, but by this time Vera had made contact, independently, with the British intelligence officer at the embassy. It was true that Gabrielle had managed to see Sir Samuel Hoare and that her plan was all set to be passed on to Winston Churchill. But the whole mission was now doomed to fail, because the two women told different stories, had completely opposing aims, and yet had come from Paris with German safe-conduct passes, thus arousing the worst suspicions.

The British decided to inform London of Gabrielle's desire to see Churchill, and in the meantime to let the women stew – to see if they revealed any ulterior motive for their sudden appearance in Spain. A young Englishman, known to them only by the code name Ramon, was appointed to keep an eye on them. Perhaps with the intention of forcing some kind of rupture, some kind of disclosure, he advised Vera Bate not to associate with Gabrielle and if possible to stay elsewhere, not at the Ritz. Vera did as she was told but somewhat tactlessly reappeared at the Ritz in the company of an Italian diplomat, the Marchese di San Felice, who had been fired from the corps for refusing to side with Mussolini. Seeing Vera in the company of an obvious British ally, Gabrielle is supposed to have held out her tea cup to Vera with the words, 'English prisoners are always given free tea'.

From that moment on, Vera saw that her future in any scheme that was in Gabrielle's control was going to be bad news for her. Her desire to get herself back to Italy was now her sole aim. As it happened, 'Operation Hat' was nearing its collapse due to circumstances beyond Gabrielle's control. Winston Churchill had been taken ill, total bed rest was ordered by his doctors, and in the end, he went to Marrakesh to convalesce.

Gabrielle had no alternative but to return to Paris. Vera, however, did not join her. She stayed behind in Madrid, waiting for the British to secure her safe return to Italy. She had to wait a long time, for the dubious circumstances of her arrival with Gabrielle, on German orders, caused the British to treat her with caution.

Rome was liberated in July 1944, but Vera Bate was not allowed to go home until January 1945.

Gabrielle never forgave Vera for not supporting her in her plan. The fact that she had caused Vera's imprisonment and separation from her husband and country-by-marriage, stood as nothing beside her own frustrated schemes. She even wrote a bitter letter to Vera on which she concluded '. . . I am surprised to see that the years have not taught you to be more trusting and less ungrateful. Times as cruel and sad as these should be able to work that sort of miracle.'

Coco's dressing-table

It was not Vera who was misguided, but Gabrielle who, as the years rolled by, lost all sense of proportion and saw anyone protecting their own interests, rather than hers, as a traitor. Her delusion in the matter of 'Operation Hat' had yet further to run before its course ended. On her return to Paris, she saw her only task as the necessity to go direct to Berlin and report on what she had tried to achieve and how she had failed – to Schellenberg himself.

So with her customary nerve and energy, Gabrielle, in her sixtieth year, made the hazardous journey to Berlin. It was an utterly mad thing to do, and the conclusion is inescapable that she went to Berlin with the sole intention of securing Schellenberg's admiration – to justify her actions and come out of the affair with yet another conquest, not necessarily sexual, but with a victory for her spirit, her powers of persuasion.

There is no record of what took place between them. At the very least a friendship was formed, for many years later it was to Gabrielle that Schellenberg turned for help which was not denied him. Perhaps that was based entirely on fear and likely blackmail.

Gabrielle paid a high price for her vanity. When Paris was liberated, she was arrested by the 'Fifis', the officials of the Clean-Up Committee which investigated collaborators with the Nazi regime, at eight o'clock one morning. Three hours later, she was released and was back at work in her salon by noon. Someone high up must have put in a word for her, because there were many people who had done less than Gabrielle, and lost their lives. What that protection was, no one knows. It is possible that the Duke of Westminster supported Gabrielle in her plan from the start. It is also possible that, while not being directly involved, he interceded on her behalf at the moment of crisis. It is equally possible (and some witnesses in the village of Garches, where her villa Bel Respiro was situated, bear testimony to the fact) that Churchill himself traced Chanel at the end of the war, to ensure her safety. Pierre Galante quotes a friend, who said of Gabrielle: 'She was never a morally lax woman. In extreme moments she might be ignoble, but lax, never. She stood firm and never let other friends be compromised like her. She once said to me that she'd been scared out of her wits, but that she had overcome that fear. That's real courage.'

Gabrielle was not the only one of her circle to be challenged by the authorities. Serge Lifar, her old friend from the days of the Ballets Russes under Diaghilev, was denounced for continuing to work at the Opéra – on the grounds that he had provided entertainment for high-ranking Nazis. Eventually he too was exonerated.

Whatever happened, the outcome was that Gabrielle Chanel chose to live in exile in Switzerland, although she returned occasionally to France, to her villa La Pausa, in the summer months. She was not alone. In exile she revived her relationship with the German officer-spy, Spatz. Nor was she without funds, for the proceeds of the foreign sales of Chanel No. 5 were salted away in a Swiss bank.

When the Americans liberated Paris, there was one souvenir of the city they all wanted. An average GI only had to enter a perfumery and hold up five fingers, to buy Chanel's classic. Through the war, the Wertheimers had been selling No. 5 through American PXs. No other perfume sold as well as Chanel's creation.

In 1946 Chanel decided on a new ruse to defeat the Wertheimer brothers. She began manufacturing and marketing new perfumes under the 'Mlle Chanel' label, competing with her erstwhile partners. She even went so far as to produce a new image, packaging her samples in red cartons. What the Wertheimers did could not be fought against in the French courts, but in America minority shareholders were better protected at law. Her lawyer, René de Chambrun, finally managed to get an out-of-court settlement with the Wertheimers who agreed to pay her legal costs, but secured an agreement that they and only they could manufacture and sell the 'red perfumes'. Even then she did not rest. She tried another industrialist in the USA willing to manufacture her 'red perfumes' – a man completely unaware of the US court's ruling. This defiance of the courts came to nothing.

But she battled on. Gabrielle created another magnificent perfume, which René de Chambrun had tested by an expert 'nose'. He declared that it was one better than Chanel No. 5. Then Gabrielle established that she could quite legally manufacture this perfume in Switzerland and simply 'send it' to some friends. Of course, these friends happened to be some of the most influential retailers and her firm supporters in the USA: Sam Goldwyn, Bernard Gimpel, and Nieman Marcus. But the Wertheimers could not let this defiance pass. The perfume was never launched. After protracted negotiations new terms were agreed between the parties, giving Gabrielle a much more substantial income from the sale of the Parfums Chanel products, at the time her share being in the region of a million dollars a year. At the age of sixty-five Gabrielle Chanel became one of the wealthiest women in the world.

Riches were not the answer. Gabrielle lived a secluded existence. Spatz was frequently at her side, and one wonders whether she kept him company out of guilt at their unacceptable relationship during the war years, or merely out of a desperate fear of loneliness. They lived for a while in Switzerland at Villars-sur-Ollon. Sometimes they went to Italy. The friends who visited her were just the sort of companions that old age provides: her dentist, her doctor, an oculist. Boredom was the keynote of her existence. Eventually she tired even of Spatz, and sent him away. He continued to receive an allowance from her – was this a way of buying his silence? The only other person who received a regular income from her during these post-war years was her nephew, André Pallasse, whose health continued to be poor.

Gabrielle moved restlessly from hotel to hotel in Switzerland. She lunched or dined with friends in restaurants, and shopped. She was hardly ever drawn into a conversation about her past career, her work as a couturier. It was a chapter closed.

Meanwhile, the 'Modelhut' episode continued to threaten her anonymous peace. In 1945 Schellenberg had been sent for judgement by the court of Nuremberg. Such was the enormity and complexity of the crimes to be heard that he was held prisoner without trial for three years. A lot of Gabrielle's money was used to buy silence, to prevent any detail of the episode from reaching hostile ears.

As if that were not enough to cause Gabrielle anxiety, even misery, her greatest friends began to desert her, this time not by choice but in death. Vera Bate died in 1947, after only a brief reunion with her husband. She and Gabrielle were never reconciled. José María Sert died that same year, and then, gravest of all, came the death of Misia at the age of eighty-five, in 1950, in Paris. She had suffered from drug addiction in her later years, and lost her sight, but was at least reconciled with her husband, the greatest love of her life. Gabrielle had to pay her respects to her oldest friend. This accounted for one of her few post-war trips to the French capital. She laid out her confidante in the old manner, smoothing away the wrinkles in her skin with ice-cubes, painting her lips with a touch of red, bringing back the image of Misia at the height of her influence, in the heyday of the Ballets Russes, when Renoir had found her his favourite muse. The body was dressed all in white, as Diaghilev would have wished, and white flowers were ordered for the funeral.

In 1951 Etienne Balsan died in a car crash, like Boy Capel. On visits to her nephew's château de Lambeyc, Gabrielle had often met up with her old friend, who had a house nearby. She wore his amethyst ring to the end of her days, on a chain around her neck.

PARIS
REVISITED

Other stars now shone in the firmament of Paris. 1947 saw the birth of the 'New Look', the conception of Christian Dior, who quite rightly judged that, after the war, women wanted to look wholly feminine again. Crinoline skirts to mid-shin, waspie waists achieved with corseting, and high, high heels so that the wearers would wobble and mince – in other words, be captive in their bodies once again. Glamour, escapism and abundance were on offer to women who had been limited to a set number of buttons and a prescribed length of hem due to government regulations. Of course it helped that Christian Dior was backed by Marcel Boussac, a textile magnate with considerable financial power and an ambition to stimulate the French luxury textile industry so that it could regain its supremacy, post-war. During the hostilities, mass production had developed apace (the large-scale manufacture of uniforms led to great advances in machinery and pattern cutting) but Christian Dior almost single-handedly restored Paris as the arbiter of fashion.

No doubt Gabrielle watched the new generation of couturiers rise to fame with mixed feelings. Dior's opening had attracted many of her closest friends: Count Etienne de Beaumont, Christian Bérard, Michel de Brunhoff from *Vogue*. Another American fashion expert, Carmel Snow, coined the name, 'New Look'.

Coco said: 'Dressing women is not a man's job. They dress women badly because they despise them.' It is significant that the post-war creators of fashion were men: Christian Dior, Cristobal Balenciaga, Jacques Fath and Marcel Rochas. They imposed their dreams on women, whereas the earlier generation, all woman, created wearable, innovative, long-lasting designs – women like Vionnet, Schiaparelli, and Chanel herself. Madeleine Vionnet had introduced the bias-cut, and was the first to design a dress that slipped over the head. Elsa Schiaparelli played with new synthetic fabrics, brought fantasy and fun to *haute couture*, and successfully launched zip-fasteners. But Gabrielle Chanel brought wearability, achievable chic, and democratised fashion years before ready-to-wear was ever realised.

It is conceivable that even if Gabrielle had wanted to re-open her salon immediately after the war, she knew she could not put herself back in the public eye while her wartime activities were still likely to be discovered and cause her great embarrassment. The threat of exposure through Schellenberg's trial hung over Gabrielle's head until 1949, when he was finally sentenced to six years' imprisonment, 'the lightest penalty this Court has inflicted' as recorded by the historian Alan Bullock. While in captivity Schellenberg had some sort of contact with Gabrielle, for a letter dated 11th April 1950, to Theodor Momm, the original go-between in the 'Modelhut' affair, reveals their continuing relationship.

'Dear Sir, I thank you with all my heart for your Christmas wishes and especially for passing on those of "Modelhut". Please convey my special thanks to her. Tell her also, in suitable terms, how very much I should have enjoyed taking part in that little reunion.'

On his release from prison in 1951, Schellenberg went to Switzerland and made contact with Gabrielle directly. She sent him money – was it out of kindness or in order to ensure his silence? Gabrielle had a long history of buying silence, dating back to the Twenties and those pensions for her brothers. Schellenberg was considering writing his memoirs, in keeping with many other confidants of Hitler, who found a large market for their confessions. His plan was foiled by the Swiss authorities, who requested that he leave the country. On the testimony of his wife, Gabrielle financed the Schellenbergs' retreat to a house in the Italian lakes.

That was not the end of her worries. The publisher with whom Schellenberg was negotiating took an unscrupulous interest in his relationship with the famous Mlle Chanel. Gabrielle was forced to part with a large sum of money to silence the man.

Schellenberg died, demoralised by his loss of power and influence, in 1952. Even this brought no relief to Gabrielle, for his widow continued to struggle to have his memoirs published. She needed the money. In her efforts to wrest the copyright from the hands of certain Swiss individuals, she tried to involve Gabrielle in the legal battle.

Gabrielle had one last ally, the final link with the 'Modelhut' operation: Theodor Momm. He was the cavalry captain who had first presented her plan to Schellenberg in Berlin, and who had secured the release of her nephew. He came to her rescue. His words are interesting testimony to the admiration and loyalty that Gabrielle could arouse, even in a purported enemy. In a letter to Schellenberg's widow, he wrote:

'In the present state of affairs, one must not hold a grudge against that generous and helpful woman. She knows how much more exposed she is than anyone else, and does not want to bring up the events or turbulence either of the wartime or of the immediate post-war period again.'

The 'Modelhut' affair lingered on and on, a permanent nightmare that even death seemed not to conquer. Nine months after Schellenberg's demise, Spatz, still then Gabrielle's lover, visited the Nazi widow and asked for an official document to confirm her husband's death. Perhaps Gabrielle was being threatened with blackmail from another source. Perhaps Spatz himself was up to no good – he had done deals behind partners' backs before. Perhaps Gabrielle had reached such a pitch of neurosis about the compromising interlude that only the possession of official documents would convince her that the menace no longer had any force. There were many other documents of her own background that she had paid to have disappear. Once a person starts running from the past, it never eludes the fugitive, but always threatens to return.

1953 was a turning point in Gabrielle's eventful life. The Duke of Westminster died, breaking a significant link with her Parisian career and her personal ambitions. (Ironically, Bend Or never succeeded in siring a male heir who survived, in four marriages, and on his death the title passed to a cousin.) In that same year, Gabrielle sold her villa, La Pausa.

Incredibly, at seventy years of age, Gabrielle decided to return to Paris and reopen her salon.

This was partly due to her continuing battles with the Wertheimers, over her 'red perfumes', which she was threatening to distribute in the USA at the time. Eventually the court's ruling was that Gabrielle should be paid substantial damages by the Wertheimers for *not* going ahead with the manufacture and sales of her 'red perfumes'.

However, in 1947 Gabrielle had gone to America and discovered that she was still famous and acceptable to the public there. (This trip is further evidence of protection from high places, for visas to get into the USA were hard to come by after the war.) Eternally creative in mischief, Gabrielle had begun exploring the possibility of finding an American manufacturer who would produce a line of her designs in America – she consulted the then editor of American *Vogue*, Carmel Snow, on the subject. Such tactics succeeded in forcing the Wertheimers to help finance her début – it was not, as many people thought at the time, a publicity stunt to boost the sales of Chanel No. 5. The Bourjois company decided it was better to entertain the enemy than allow her to go elsewhere and cause trouble.

Besides, even some elements in France were less hostile to Gabrielle, for her reputation was sustained by the frequent mention of her past life in the pages of writers like Jean Cocteau and Paul Morand. A younger generation of French women had a curiosity about her life.

Gabrielle knew that the American market would be the most important one for couture and persuaded herself that her reputation there would bring her many customers.

Another cogent argument for reopening was that the reign of the great men designers, Dior, Balenciaga, Fath, Heim, was beginning to decline, for it seemed not to accept the realities of the new world. Fashion had to keep pace with social change, and their élitist, complicated designs were not easy to turn into high street big sellers. There was even talk that couture was 'dead' or, at least, becoming progressively less relevant. Women were beginning to be bored with the tyranny of the designers, their dictates as to what length a hem should be (and naturally making it move up and down from year to year). As Coco said: 'If I've got a big head, should I throw myself in the Seine because these messieurs have decreed that this year, heads will "be small"? *La mode* has become absurd, the couturiers have forgotten there are women inside these dresses. The majority of women dress for men and want to be admired. But they must be able to move, get into a car, without splitting their seams! Clothes should have a natural shape!'

This line of thought convinced Gabrielle that the time was right for a return to her basically unchanged concept of fashion, which was not about fashion at all, but about style. Fashion dates, style never does. As Raymond Barthès the sociologist said: 'Chanel's creations challenge the very idea of fashion. Fashion . . . is based on a fierce feeling for the times. Every year, fashion destroys the thing it has just adored, and adores the thing that it will destroy; the rejected fashion of the year past could speak to the victorious fashion of the present year with those most hostile words that the dead convey to the living, and which can be seen sometimes on tombstones: "I was yesterday the thing you are today, you will be tomorrow the thing I am today." Chanel's work does not concern itself – or at least only minimally concerns itself – with this annual vendetta. Chanel works always on the same model which she merely varies from year to year, just as one varies a theme in music. Her work says (and she herself confirms) that there is an eternal beauty in woman which may be transmitted by the history of art; indignantly she rejects the use of those throw-away materials (such as paper) which people in the USA sometimes use in the making of clothes. Chanel makes a precious attribute out of the very thing which says no to fashion: a quality of endurance.'

But by far the most important and personal reason for her comeback was that Gabrielle was stultifyingly bored. There was no man in her life, no aim, no challenge. (Shortly after her re-launch, Marlene Dietrich, a longstanding client, came to order from her once more. 'Why did you begin again?' she asked. 'Because I was dying of boredom,' Gabrielle replied. 'You too!' exclaimed Marlene. They found her original orders and measurements in the ancient paperwork of the house. None of her measurements had altered.)

Perhaps the very hostility of the French urged Gabrielle to conquer them publicly. Besides, the extreme bitterness of the late Forties, when accusations of

Chanel and her models, 1962

collaboration flew thickly through Paris, had died down, leaving her a little hope
that bygones could be bygones.

In 1950 Gabrielle tested public opinion by writing a feature for *Paris-Match*,
on her beliefs about women and fashion. The article was to be a dress rehearsal
for a book she would publish, *Chanel par Chanel* – a title reminiscent of her great
friend Misia's own publication. The article she wrote, 'Coco's advice on how to
stay young', is a strange mix of practical sense, esoteric opinion, and plain
eccentricity. For example: she rejects any notion that women should keep themselves fit by taking regular exercise. She suggests a study of 'repose' as opposed
to 'boredom'. The only exercise she recommends is to make a series of bunny
hops, a positively dotty notion. Food is discussed with the same odd strictures:
no eating of white meat like poultry; spend a whole week every three months
eating nothing but vegetables; in all, subject the body to a series of 'shocks' or
surprises, in terms of diet, to keep it in good form. The article certainly succeeds in
reminding the general public of her individuality, and her unorthodox, challenging
mentality!

Gabrielle Chanel worked hard for that first collection, re-entering the world of

couture with considerably less support than she had had in the past. Whereas she once had several thousand employees, she was now pared down to an essential 350. The empty rue Cambon workrooms upstairs were cleaned up, rusting sewing machines thrown out, and bare-floored workspaces suddenly filled with another army of dedicated little stitching girls, bringing the old house back to life with the sound of their laughter, and the rustle of wonderful fabrics.

For her comeback in 1953, she began work with only one model and one fitter. Her method never changed. She hardly ever drew sketches of her designs, preferring to examine a prototype on a model girl, who would then have to stand still for hours at a stretch, while Gabrielle cut, re-pinned, re-draped the embryonic garment, until she had it moulded exactly to her taste. She was ruthless about her mannequins, needing to be inspired by a girl's particular beauty, but expecting that one to remain silent, co-operative, and above all to show a patience and stamina equal to her own self-critical workpace. (Coco: 'There are some girls I simply can't work on, gargoyles.')

To be a Chanel mannequin, a girl had to mould herself entirely in the image that her mistress wanted of her. She had to learn how to walk, stand still (hips jutting forward, hands in pockets, a boyish stance like that of Gabrielle herself), how to apply her make-up, fix her hair, and above all, how to say little.

Her loyal *directrice* Mme Raymond would hang a special pair of scissors on a long tape round Gabrielle's neck, and she would lean forward over each garment in turn. 'All you have to do is subtract,' she said. Or later, 'Keep working till you hate the sight of it. Such stinginess, you can't move that sleeve – anyone would think the object was to be uncomfortable!' As ever, the murmured monologue continued, growing steadily more obscure and compulsive as the years passed. By the end of the session, the air would be heavy with nervous exhaustion, but Gabrielle would get up from the floor, as fresh and neat as when she had begun, hours before. It was an exercise of will that brought her gratification.

She liked to use the colours of nature, hating anything that spoke too loudly of the synthetic. She was no doubt thinking of her arch-rival Schiaparelli (still in business) when she spoke of a vivid pink, the kind always associated with its creator, Scap: 'A pink that sets your teeth on edge! I take refuge in beige because it's natural. Not dyed. Red, because it's the colour of blood and we've so much inside us it's only right to show a little outside.'

Tension mounted as the date of her first showing came closer. It was a major event in the fashion world, taking place on 5th February 1954; five had always been her lucky number. Balenciaga sent her camellias in a heart shape. 'Flowers to put on a coffin,' Coco scoffed. 'People shouldn't be in such a hurry to bury me.' There were many, many enemies, sitting on the edge of their gilt chairs, waiting and hoping that she would fail. The first model girl appeared in a navy blue cardigan suit, superstitiously called 'Number 5'. As *Le Figaro* next day put it, 'It was touching. It was like being back in 1925.'

The verdict of the press internationally was harsh. There was nothing new happening at the rue Cambon salon; Coco Chanel had lost her touch. The vituperation was shamefully remorseless. These words from the French newspaper *Combat* are typical:

'Even as usually well-informed sources whispered that she was re-opening her house in order to further the publicity for her perfumes, Chanel was busily denying this, saying that it was only her revulsion at the bad taste of today's Paris dressmakers that had impelled her to emerge from her pleasant retirement. And the eagle eyes of this Cassandra, made new by plastic surgery, were sparkling. . . .In her games of the future we saw not the future but a disappointing reflection of the past, into which a pretentious little black figure was disappearing with giant steps.'

Even her old friends the English did not welcome her return. The *Daily Express* called the show a fiasco, the *Daily Mail* a flop. Privately Gabrielle was heard saying that perhaps they were right, perhaps she was out of touch.

A remarkable gesture came from the one source she least expected to give help. Pierre Wertheimer, her arch-enemy, came to the house. These two people had battled for years, like a brother and sister, who pick at each other continually, but gang up if anyone outside should criticise them. Coco liked to refer to Pierre as 'Bonjour Tristesse', punning on the title of Françoise Sagan's best-selling novel and the name of Wertheimer's parent company, Bourjois. Later that night he walked Gabrielle back to her room at the Ritz, listening to her discouraged words, hearing her consider giving up. 'No,' he said. 'You're right to go on. You're right.' For perhaps the first time in her life, Gabrielle turned to him and said 'Thank you'.

The story of her comeback is best told by one of the people who helped achieve it, Bettina Ballard.

'I was covering the Paris collections as *Vogue*'s fashion editor at the time and I observed the reactions of the press around me at the opening. The editors of French *Vogue*, with whom Chanel had continued to feud up to the time she closed her doors during the war, hated the collection, as did most of the press and buyers, with the exception of her friends at *Paris-Match* and *Marie-Claire*. Lord & Taylor saw a return to the navy-and-white jersey look in the collection and bought; B. Altman bought; Hattie Carnegie, for old time's sake, bought one – altogether about six things. I photographed three full pages of Chanel models and *Vogue* backed up my fashion judgement by opening the March issue with them. The frontispiece showed Marie-Hélène Arnaud, a completely unknown mannequin, whom Chanel had created in her own image, leaning against a wall in a navy jersey suit with her hands plunged deep in her pockets, her tucked white lawn blouse buttoned on to the easy skirt under her loose open jacket, her navy cuffs rolled back to show the white ones, and a navy straw sailor with ribbon streamers on the back of her head. I had owned practically the identical suit before the war and the whole look was as familiar to me as "Swanee River". I wanted this costume for myself – I had missed comfortable, reliable young clothes like this, and I was sure that other women would want them too, if they saw them.'

Bettina Ballard continued to beat the drum for Chanel when she went back to America, so much so that by the time of Chanel's next showing in the autumn of 1954, many individuals in the fashion world were vying to be the one who had 'rediscovered' Chanel. Before long, copies of Chanel suits were being bought in every major city of America and Europe – with no direct benefit to Gabrielle, beyond the intense satisfaction of being proved right. She was flattered by plagiarism. 'I like fashion to go down into the street, but I can't accept that it should originate there,' she said. As Bettina Ballard concluded: 'She will certainly go down in history as the only couturier who spanned the taste of almost half a century without ever changing her basic conception of clothes.'

The cost of supporting Chanel was quite onerous to the Wertheimers. The perfume sales did not leap up as various people had predicted – not at once. But Coco Chanel was fast becoming an institution, a vital form of public relations. It was unthinkable that she should not go on. The final arrangement was that Bourjois bought the rights to everything to do with Chanel, paid for everything, including the cost of her rooms at the Ritz, even her domestic staff, telephones, stamps, the lot. She was left to do exactly what she liked in the rue Cambon. Hiring and firing staff, ordering fabrics and so on was entirely in her hands. Only the financial side of the House was to be managed by the head company. In return she was to collaborate in the making of perfumes with the expectation of hundreds of thousands of royalties each year. This agreement was not prompted entirely out of altruism. Devilish to the last, Coco occasionally threatened to sell her couture house to an outside buyer – who might not keep up the exceptional standard of work, or might take the house in another direction. In a sense, the Wertheimers needed Gabrielle to produce the authentic, everlasting style she had developed, as if she were the figurehead on the prow of their company vessel, a symbol of enduring quality.

At its height the revived salon had eight workrooms. Four of these were the 'creative workshops' where new designs were devised. The other four provided

Coco at work in her reopened salon in rue Cambon

the models sold to customers. Each held about thirty people, all the way up the scale in the traditional couture way, from little apprentices to qualified specialists, each room under the management of a *première* or tailor. Fortunately the Occupation had not damaged the impressive tradition of craft.

One of Gabrielle's greatest talents lay in her immaculate sense of colour, and her intense, physical enjoyment of textiles. She approached choosing her fabrics like an artist mixes paints. Sometimes she would go up to the studio to pick out material, but then oddly would decide she was not in the mood, and instead spend the time telling anecdotes about her past life. When the right mood came upon her, she would roll out the textiles, touch them sensuously, visualising a new design from within the raw cloth. Sometimes she would crush flowerheads, mix the petals on a fabric surface, to show the colouring effect she wanted.

When Gabrielle wanted to create a new model, her method never varied throughout her career. She would describe it in great detail, gesturing with her hands, demonstrating with fingers waving through the air, exactly how it should be constructed. No sketches were made. The 'hands', cutters and seamstresses, would work up the object, which then came to Gabrielle. She would rip sleeves out, recut armholes, tear off collars, ease the skirts – hers was the only imagination that could be realised. A garment would go back and forth several times for reconstruction, before she was satisfied. Her *première* of the *premières*, Mme Manon, entered the salon as an apprentice in 1933, and came back to the reopened house in 1953. 'Mademoiselle always created by herself . . . not a thing could come from us. And if anyone added on some frippery she would say – "Look at that – as if I'd allow them to do that . . . people add bits on, but that's not elegance. Elegance is in the line."'

'In old age, elegance and fastidiousness are a form of dignity. A young woman shouldn't be elaborate – it's so dowdy,' Coco would affirm.

Colette's picture of 1935 was just as applicable when Coco was seventy.

'Mlle Chanel is a little black bull . . . with a little dark curly tuft of hair, like the proud crest of a bull calf, which tumbles on her forehead down to her eyebrows, and dances to every movement of her head.

'There she is, kneeling before her materials, between two great bolts of jersey, like pillars, with a great beam of printed silk above her. Long rolls of satin whisper as they are unfolded, and below, the chaos of rubble, little wisps of bits and pieces which make not a single sound as they are scattered about.'

Colette describes Gabrielle as a Delilah in a collapsing temple to fashion. However, there was no Samson to ensnare.

In a remarkable revival of energy, Gabrielle Chanel continued with her work, producing new collections twice a year for a further seventeen years. The tight-lipped, aged old woman in exile was revivified as an exceptional figure of energy and beauty – photographic portraits testify to the resurgence of warmth in her features.

Not everything about her revival brought her happiness. Apart from the death of close friends and of the great artistic figures of her younger days, there were the burdensome dilemmas of boredom or loneliness. She was irascible, did not suffer fools gladly, but at the same time hated her own company. Gabrielle entertained in her rooms above the salon at rue Cambon. Her staff and few close friends were made embarrassingly conscious of her fear of being alone. She would befriend someone, say a model, and expect that girl to be available to her as a companion, night after night, until she tired of the friendship and transferred her affections to a new 'favourite'. When the guests had finished supper someone would accompany Gabrielle back to the Hôtel Ritz. She would detain her companion on the pavement outside, putting off as long as possible the moment when she would have to go upstairs to her own quarters, a tiny salon, bathroom and bedroom.

Her usual routine was to wake early, take a simple breakfast of porridge and black coffee. She would then stay in bed going through the day's mail, dealing most with demands for financial assistance. She would rise at about one o'clock and then go to the rue Cambon salon. At the end of her day she would return, as late as possible, and watch television or read books, to fill up the silent hours of her solitude.

Coco would say: 'If my friends tease me for talking non-stop, it's because they don't realise I'm terrified at the thought of being bored by other people. If I ever die it will be of boredom.'

Note the phrase, 'If I ever die'. Just as she seldom went into the workrooms, afraid of too close contact with poverty, so now she kept away from any signs of mortality. She hated to have anyone ill around her – anyone on her staff who required medical treatment of a serious nature was in danger of being laid off. Gabrielle was not preparing herself for death at all, though she carried a little note in her handbag, stating that if she were to fall ill, a priest should be summoned to give her the last rites. This was a poignant return to the religion of her youth, a complete volte-face on the Coco who could not remember prayers while the Germans invaded France.

Gabrielle was not only battling against loneliness, but against an increasing tendency to repulse those few friends who were prepared to be close to her. Claude Baillen, a psycho-analyst who later wrote a book about Gabrielle, was one such; Serge Lifar, Diaghilev's collaborator, was another. Coco's tongue was vicious; she often said unforgivable things behind the back of someone who had

Coco, tired at the end of a day, 1962

been kind to her. Many friends such as Georges Auric actively avoided contact with her, preferring to remember the vivacious genius of fashion he had known many years before. Gabrielle hated to be beholden to anyone, and suffered dreadfully from the acknowledgment that she really needed people in this ultimate situation. Her dependency irritated her, and made her destroy the one thing she wanted: love.

She loathed her state. She began to say to anyone prepared to keep her company that her life was a total failure because she had not had children or kept a man's love. She reverted to the most anti-feminist views on the relationship between men and women:

'A woman who's not loved is no woman. A woman who's not loved is a woman who's lost. The only thing for her is to die.'

In an interview given in 1966, she advised women to lead a conventional life if they wanted to find happiness. 'If not, they need heroic courage and in the end will pay a terrible price – solitude. There is nothing worse for a woman. Solitude can help a man to realise himself but it is annihilation to a woman. It is better to stay with a husband – even if he becomes fat and deadly dull – than to be alone.'

She ascribed traditional roles to men and women in relationships. The sad truth is that these sayings are probably just as applicable today as they were when spoken:

'Women have to be the strongest beings on earth. Men always expect women to be like a little pillow, on which they can lay their head. . . . They have a nostalgia for the mother who raised them. Women have to keep telling them, all the time, that they really do exist. Truly, it's the women who are the strong ones.'

Even her great achievement, at having built up an empire entirely on her own creativity, brought her no satisfaction. 'Money's not becoming to women. It makes them think they can do everything.' Did Gabrielle really believe that it was her money that gave her too much power, and drove men away? She had always, even when poor, been wilful.

The only time these negative thoughts abated was while she was at work. Then she became so transported by creation that she experienced respite, an interlude of peace in her heart. But when the work was over, the thoughts came back at once.

'My life is a failure. Don't you think it's a failure, to work as I work, under this lamp? I've cried a lot. And if I've found refuge in dresses and coats. . . . When you've lost those you adored. . . .

'I've wept so much. Now I don't cry any more. When you don't cry, it's because you don't believe in happiness any more.'

Sometimes she would divert herself by playing games with her underlings. The salon became a harem, and at times, in the early 1960s, the names of the staff read like a listing from the *Almanach de Gotha* (the French *Debrett's*). Gabrielle knew the personal details of everyone's life, and expected to be first in their concern. If a girl dared turn down an evening date with Mlle Coco, she would be ignored for several days.

Every morning, the salon girls would post someone as look-out at the front door, who would pass the word back when Gabrielle was about to arrive – and what sort of mood she was in. And the last thing the girls would do before Gabrielle's appearance was to touch up their lipstick – for she hated young women who paid too little attention to their appearance.

Certain things brought her great pleasure – or at least diversion. First there were her horses. She bought a foal and a filly at the yearlings' sale at Deauville. Owning her own horses! It was a far cry from the Royallieu days, and no doubt the achievement of a long-desired fantasy. Her racing colours were, of course, red for the shirt and hat, and white armbands. Her favourite horse, Romantica, did well, winning her first race. But what Gabrielle liked best was when her horse beat one from Pierre Wertheimer's stables. He did win the Epsom Derby once. Gabrielle thought he would be insufferable after that. When he came to share his good fortune, she pretended not to know anything about it – and then worked up false anger that he had not brought her the news sooner!

Baiting 'Bonjour Tristesse' had become a regular hobby. On one occasion she was piqued to discover that she was being taxed as a 'spinster'. This unattractive nomenclature drove her once more to make mischief. 'If Wertheimer wants me to appear in the grand enclosure, at the Grand Prix de Deauville, let him pay my taxes. I won't go otherwise. No – let him also pay my Swiss taxes. I never go to the weigh-ins. You meet too many snobs. I go to the show-ring. So – let him make the gesture!'

Then in 1958, there was the whole of the Chambre Syndicale de la Haute Couture Parisienne to bait too. Gabrielle wrote to the then president, Raymond Barbas (head of the long-hated rival's company, Patou), resigning from the union. Difficulties had arisen the year before when Gabrielle had allowed some of her latest models to be photographed in advance of the 'press date' set by the couturier's union, the Chambre. The official reasons for the embargo were numerous: a set date put all the newspapers on an equal footing with regard to stories. The ruling also protected those manufacturers who came to Paris to buy *toiles* – exact copies of the model gowns made up in cheaper muslin which provide the full data for versions to be made as ready-to-wear. The premature release of the actual models enabled other manufacturers to whizz up copies without going to the expense of buying a *toile*. Also, there were in Paris numerous smaller couturiers practically dependent on the sale of models and *toiles* who would be cut out of the market, if big-name designers could be so easily and directly plagiarised.

Gabrielle Chanel of course dismissed all these arguments. She had always firmly believed that to be copied was to be paid a compliment. And she added defiantly: 'Besides, the best proof that *"la mode"* is not made to be set in aspic, is that it should go out of date. As quickly as possible!'

The union despaired (although in fact, Gabrielle went on paying her dues to this illustrious organisation on the quiet). Still, her behaviour totally supported her line of argument – Gabrielle was never a hypocrite. For example, a young dressmaker from the provinces wrote to her naïvely explaining that she could not afford to travel to Paris and get into the big collections at show time. Was it possible for Mlle Chanel to let her come in from time to time to see the latest directions of her work? Gabrielle responded with equal frankness: of course she could come. On another occasion, she allowed a group of nuns to bring their pupils in – no doubt much amused, in her private thoughts, about those other nuns who had trained her, Julia and Antoinette so well, back in the days of Moulins.

A lack of hypocrisy was also the reason she declined to accept the *Légion d'Honneur* before the war, on the grounds that it had already been received by other designers. She did, however, turn a blind eye to the fact that Dior had already been granted the American 'Oscar' for fashion, the Nieman Marcus Award, and agreed to accept the honour as 'the most influential creator of twentieth-century fashion'. She travelled to Dallas for the presentation ceremony, in 1957, and journeyed on to New Orleans, to accept the keys of the city – at the age of seventy-four. In 1963 the *Sunday Times* in London honoured her with the title, 'Fashion Immortal' but, once more, she refused to receive the award in person, not deigning to be ranked alongside anyone else in her field.

On the 1957 trip to America, Gabrielle was guest of honour at the Fashion Group import show in New York. Bettina Ballard describes Gabrielle's reaction at this event: 'Before I introduced her, she begged off speaking, even in French, on the grounds that she had never in all of her designing years spoken in public, that her stomach would drop, her knees wobble, and her voice disappear. This woman, who is famous for her open-water-tap stream of words, was speechless before the mammoth cheering audience, although her monkey grin was far more expressive than words.'

Bettina goes on to describe Gabrielle's utter shock at the kinds of clothes other designers were producing, giving the impression that she had never exposed herself to other couturiers' work in such detail before. Bettina is surprised, but it is easy to see that Gabrielle had to insulate herself from other ideas, other directions, in order to keep the spark of inspiration alive in herself. She was outside fashion, in a sense, impervious to changing ideas in dress.

Among the many begging letters and importunists at her door, there were now many writers, all of whom she confused by telling lies about her age, her background, her love affairs and her friendships. Her supposed reason was this: 'One couldn't speak of oneself, or almost never. People should guess you. If the soul issues forth anywhere, if it listens and talks, it's on our tongue. The mouth is our most sensitive part.' However, one has the impression that there was nearly always some eager scribe just behind her, grasping a tape-recorder, anxiously recording all her frenzied murmurings for posterity – an exasperating experience considering Coco's deceptive convolutions. She disliked analysis of personal motives, involving too much navel-gazing. Coco: 'Before, no one had *complexes*. They were called vices. I'd rather have people with vices than people with complexes.'

One by one the writers entered her lair above the salon in the rue Cambon, her extraordinary sitting room filled with mirrors, black fur rugs, gilt boxes, exquisite Chinese jade objects, a Greek marble Venus, statues of blackamoors, crystal chandeliers and, in the ante-room, the essential coromandel screens, hoping to be the one and only writer to find the truth inside Coco. Marcel Haedrich, editor-in-chief of *Marie-Claire* magazine, first brought to light the details of Gabrielle's birth and her family origins. Pierre Galante wrote in great detail about her business affairs, in *Les Années Chanel*. Claude Baillen, a personal friend, wrote a sympathetic portrait of these years of her revival, in *Chanel Solitaire*. Edmonde Charles-Roux got closest to a complete portrait of the woman who was a great personal friend of her mother's, in *L'Irregulière* published in 1974 and translated into English two years later, under the title *Chanel*. This contained the amazing story of Gabrielle's wartime adventures. (Charles-Roux was also a former editor of French *Vogue* and a winner of the Prix Goncourt, but even she, according to Philippa Toomey reviewing her book in *The Times*, London, was forced 'to embroider, to assume, to speculate'.) And Ernestine Carter, British doyenne of fashion, in *The Magic Names of Fashion* concludes, 'The result is a kind of folklore, faithfully, if not accurately, repeated in every biography . . . Chanel was creating a legend while she lived. . . .'

Another version of her life story appeared on the Broadway stage: *Coco*, in 1969 – the result of more than a decade of persuasion and negotiation on the part of Frederick Brisson. His intention was to make Coco his property, in every form, biography, play or musical comedy. In the end he got Gabrielle's agreement to a musical, with the libretto by Alan Jay Lerner, and the score by André Previn.

The greatest objection Gabrielle had was to Mr Brisson's wife, Rosalind Russell, in the leading role. 'That big horse,' said Coco. 'No.' The story goes that she suggested playing the role herself. Failing that, she grudgingly conceded that the Hepburn woman might do instead, ignoring the decades in age between them. The producers thought she meant Katharine Hepburn when in fact Coco intended Audrey to be the star! In the end, the former played the part magnificently, though the show was not a long-running Broadway best.

Any designer who tried to reproduce 'Chanel' for the stage would be courting disaster. Such was the fate of Cecil Beaton, who with some experience in these matters, explained that he had to design 'costumes, not clothes' – and also quite correctly pointed out that her own work was 'undramatic, un-theatre'. (Cecil Beaton was a notable photographer and costume designer, perhaps best known for his costuming of the films *Gigi* [1958] and *My Fair Lady* [1964].) If Gabrielle thought back to her technical defeat at the Goldwyn Studios in Hollywood, she was unwilling to admit to the truth of his remark. Mr Beaton, a noted homosexual, was summarised by Coco thus: 'He's an old lady who's got older but not better. An old maid who's committed a lot of mortal sins.'

Some writers say that she failed to attend the opening of the musical out of pique. The truth was that Gabrielle could not face up even to this sugared version of her story. She cried on hearing the libretto run through, where the theme of her solitary state was painfully explored. More to the point, she disliked the distortion of her story – that a young American designer had helped her with her comeback, which was untrue. At the time of the New York opening she was in the American Hospital at Neuilly suffering from paralysis of the right hand, which did not clear up for several months, although she continued to work with the handicap.

The years rolled by, and Gabrielle continued to produce her faultless collections. The two-tone shoes, soft mohair suits (jackets weighted with chain to make them sit perfectly), exquisitely colour-matched silk blouses, were truly variations on a well-loved fashion theme. The late Fifties saw the apogee of her popularity, but she continued to hold out against the most extraordinary fashion developments. In the 1960s, Gabrielle was amused by the antics of the 'yéyé' designers, their designation coined from a Beatles song hit. It provided her with more entertainment: classicism versus modernism was the subject of conversation. André Courrèges saw himself as 'a Ferrari to her Rolls-Royce'. Yves Saint Laurent, heir to the mantle of Dior after Marc Bohan, was a nice boy. (Coco: 'The more he copies me, the more success he will have,' or alternatively, 'The poor boy might turn out all right if he copied me and cut his hair.') Pierre Cardin was too much of a money merchant for her taste – and frankly, he took the business of licensing his

name to unseemly vulgar levels. Besides, he stole away one of her favourite clients, the actress Jeanne Moreau. Paco Rabanne (best known for his plastic dresses, designs constructed out of metal discs and chains) was referred to as 'a metallurgist'. The House of Lanvin-Castillo provoked Gabrielle to particular ire and pettiness. Antonio Castillo, a Spaniard, joined the old-established house set up by couturière Jeanne Lanvin before the First World War, in 1950. As he had worked briefly for Mlle Chanel, he fell quite naturally into her disregard. She made a point of showing her collections on the same date as Lanvin-Castillo, an act of pure spite. Yet, as Ernestine Carter commented, 'Although Chanel fulminated against them, 31 rue Cambon rocked gently with the Nouvelle Vague. Chanel's skirts rose and fell almost imperceptibly. Perhaps it was only coincidence that in 1964, the year of Courrèges's great success with trouser suits, Chanel combined her first love with her last, showing navy flap-fronted sailor pants with her typical cardigan jacket. Whatever she inhaled was exhaled in her own smoke rings.'

Enough of the performances of Coco Chanel. There were others who were privileged to see the warmer side of her nature – presumably the emotional Gabrielle who had enchanted so many and such diverse lovers. André Pallasse, her nephew, the child she and Boy Capel had educated, was the father of two daughters by his marriage to an extremely attractive Dutch woman. The elder

Coco in her apartment in rue Cambon

The Chanel 'look' 1954

girl was Marie-Hélène Arnaud – the mannequin photographed by Bettina Ballard, and the girl who best defined Gabrielle's ideal woman. For some years Gabrielle treated 'Tiny' Marie-Hélène as her possible successor. Marie-Hélène always retained an image of Gabrielle as a devoted, generous 'Aunt Coco', capable of extreme acts of affection. Inevitably, Gabrielle quarrelled with Marie-Hélène, and her hopes for a successor of her own choice came to an end.

A source of great bitterness for Gabrielle, in 1968, was the discovery that the Wertheimers had installed next door to her salon (the headquarters of the Bourjois business), a young man who was being groomed as her successor. This treachery angered Gabrielle, and made her work all the harder. Pierre Wertheimer, her ancient foe, died in 1965. At this point Gabrielle fired the lawyer who had protected her for thirty years, René de Chambrun. Instead she hired a brilliant younger man, Robert Badinter, to confront the Wertheimer organisation. He was Jewish; Gabrielle very frankly announced she did not hold that against him! He was to remain her lawyer until her death.

One more challenge to the Wertheimers: on 24th December 1970 Gabrielle insisted on launching a new perfume, called No. 19 after the date of her birth-day. The Wertheimers did not want another product to rival No. 5, perhaps reducing their overall sales. But Gabrielle won the day. No. 19 was, and is in-tended to, appeal to a younger set, and has become an outstanding success. Even at this late stage in her career, Gabrielle made decisions of marketing genius.

Towards the end of her life, Gabrielle became gradually more obsessive about her work, and more neurotic about her solitude. She began to sleep-walk, sometimes stark naked, along the corridors of the Hôtel Ritz. Eventually her maid, always called 'Jeanne' after some particularly valued predecessor, locked the apartment door each night so that she would not wander so far. 'Jeanne' slept nearby, on hand to help the transfixed Gabrielle by leading her gently back to bed. She was becoming fragile, inclined to fall and injure herself.

At other times, the life-long love of cleanliness prompted her to wash her hands, or some article of clothing, while still sleepwalking. The touch of water would wake her with a start, and in shocked secrecy, Gabrielle would find her way back to her bed. What miseries from childhood rose up from her subconscious, filling her with these sad compulsions?

On one occasion, Gabrielle rose again entranced and cut up a bath robe to make into a suit. She went even further: a gardenia, made out of the hotel bath towel, was carefully laid on the lapel of her creation. In sleep, the same comforting creativity flowed through her. It never ceased to cast its magical, enthralling spell over her. 'I hold my world in the palm of my hand,' said Coco. Work gave her purpose, in an old age without love to provide her with any impetus. She was completely absorbed in her professional life; towards the end she stopped bothering to dress for status. She owned only two or three suits, nothing more. She left the salon late enough to use up each day, and to prevent her from fretting about a Parisian social whirl that had once, long ago, included her.

Thoughts of a spareness and sternness that matched those of Pierre Reverdy fell from her lips occasionally. Towards the end Gabrielle lost the need for that stream of consciousness that usually accompanied her work. She turned in on herself, grew silent.

All that Gabrielle had left to offer the world, and to appease her own tormented spirit, was the gift of her own hands. She was continually urged from within, to offer 'the best she had made of herself', to paraphrase her poet-lover Reverdy's words in dedicating a book to her: 'There is the best I have made of myself, with my hand.'

Reverdy died in June 1960. Only his wife Henriette and two monks from Solesmes attended his burial. Gabrielle and all the rest of his Parisian friends discovered the truth after the event, from a short item in the newspapers, as was his last wish.

Finally, at the age of eighty-eight, Gabrielle Chanel stopped work for the last time. On 10th January 1971, she went for a short walk, then returned to her bedroom. She lay down for a rest, still fully clothed. On her bedside table, an image of St Anthony of Padua, a souvenir of the first trip to Italy she had made with the Serts, shortly after Boy Capel died, and a small triple icon, a present from Stravinsky, a remembrance of their brief but valuable liaison.

It was a Sunday morning, a quite time to die, to lie down still in her neat clothes. She did not want a long-drawn-out drama with unwelcome faces at her bedside. Just a maid, who recalled for posterity Gabrielle's last words. Gasping for breath, unable to manage the syringe and medication, Sedol, that she usually gave herself, Gabrielle cried out: 'Ah, they're killing me. . . . They'll have killed me.' And then, 'So that's how you die.' Even at the end, she observed herself with a certain dispassion, as if at a distance from the event. The woman who was loved by noblemen, artists, heroes and spies, died completely alone, having outlived every one of her men.

The funeral took place at the Church of the Madeleine, the following Thursday. Her mannequins stood at the front, all dressed in Chanel clothes. The rest of her 400-strong staff stood behind. Among her personal friends, Serge Lifar, Salvador Dali, Lady Abdy, Hervé Mille, Bettina Ballard, were in attendance. So were the cream of Parisian couturiers, Balmain, Castillo, Balenciaga, Bohan, Goma, and Yves Saint Laurent. Gabrielle was laid out in her favourite working suit, and the church was filled with white flowers, as she had always loved them best. Gabrielle Chanel was buried in a cemetery in Lausanne, where she had a property and had spent many of her years in exile.

Her last collection was shown on 26th January 1971, in a strange atmosphere of respect, regret, and the knowledge that the affair was only a make-believe, without the enchanting presence of its creator, to transform it into an elegant reality.

T H E   H O U S E
O F   C H A N E L

After her death, the House of Chanel passed into the hands of Gaston Berthelot, formerly of Christian Dior New York. It was a difficult task, to follow immediately after the inimitable Gabrielle. The house began to rise in significance under the reign of Philippe Guibourgé, who was also from Christian Dior, but in Paris. He developed the ready-to-wear side of the enterprise with gratifying success, especially in the American market. Two designers who had worked closely with Chanel, Jean Cazaubon and Yvonne Dudel, managed the couture side of the business.

In 1983 Karl Lagerfeld was appointed design director for both the ready-to-wear and the couture lines, raising the name of Chanel to unprecedented heights of popularity. Another generation of women now wear the Chanel look, which stays virtually unchanged from its début in 1914. 'Coco became too refined, too distinguished at the end of her time,' Lagerfeld told Judy Rumbold of *Elle* magazine. 'When she lectured on elegance, she was *so* boring. It was more fun when she was young and cruised around being a kept woman. . . . I want to make the clothes more graphic, more fun, but with distinguished touches that change slightly from one season to the next.' In other words, Lagerfeld varies the theme, just as Gabrielle Chanel did, to perfection.

Her writer friend Maurice Sachs wrote a wonderful tribute to Gabrielle when she was at the height of her fame. His assessment of her stands the test of time.

'The power she exercised over all the women of the world; the circle with which she surrounded herself; her taste for works of art and for beautiful books; the beauty of her country houses; the splendour of her town residence; the sumptuousness of her parties; her inexhaustible generosity which made her part with her riches in all quarters; her reputation as a patron of the arts; her fortune, which people say is prodigious; her comparative isolation; the public knowledge of her marvellous, romantic conquests, all through her life – all this has contributed to make her a legend.'

All those ingredients are certainly part of the myth. But what makes her story retain its fascination, almost two decades after her death, is that she is a symbol of all that women love and fear in life. Gabrielle had the spirit to grab at the best things in experience, in every aspect. She wanted to be a great couturier, a great lover, and a mother besides. Yet she ended her life in solitude, unloved, as all women secretly know they are likely to be. Wealth and talent do not protect even the strongest of the female sex from the rigours of that final test: how to be a happy, solitary, old woman. One quality shines through all the shrewish temperament, the unreasonable egotism, the devilish intrigues that were so much a part of her existence: courage. Gabrielle Chanel pitched herself into the world with only the talent in her fingers to make her famous. It is impossible to overlook her vulnerability and the lack of security that compelled her to work all through her life. The single most worthy characteristic of this indomitable and fascinating woman was her bravery. That made her revive, time and time again, to go forward and live life to the full, whatever the setbacks and personal tragedies. Courage, and a love of beauty, which stayed with her to the very end. She was hard at work in the rue Cambon salon on the night before she died.

The Autumn Boutique Collection 1989, designed by Karl Lagerfeld, was shown in the Palais du Louvre, inside an enormous marquee, with a catwalk stretching the length of its centre. At the end of the catwalk an enclosure was erected high where the world's press jostled for position with their telephoto lenses. All round the edge of the catwalk other photographers crouched ready to capture the evolution of the Chanel look, from the hands of a master.

It was everything I had imagined a collection showing to be. The audience was filled with Chanel devotees, a sea of bobbing heads, neat hair-dos caught back with velvet bows, artificial camellias resting on top of the knot at the nape of the neck; older women in fur-lined trenchcoats; a few more dramatic characters in broad-brimmed simple hats, baroque pendant pearls swaying on their ears. A parade of Chanel suits and coats from recent years, lovingly worn and chosen by her clients for the occasion as a signal of devotion to Gabrielle Chanel's vision.

Karl Lagerfeld is just the man to carry the Chanel tradition into the 1990s. He has a wonderful sense of colour – of course there were the black dresses, long and short, filmy chiffons with enormous satin or velvet bows caught on the hipline. But there were other colours too: a scarlet as of a hunting jacket, a rich dark plum, like a fading amethyst, a ruby red, an aquamarine, a vivid emerald green, the colours of Gabrielle's jewel box. And then the earth colours, a soft deep mushroom, a baked clay brown – the favourite sombre shades of Gabrielle's disciplined palette.

How Coco would have enjoyed the witty references to her favourite details: a draped dress where the folds around the backside are signalled with a cheeky row of brass buttons; a suit with a short hussar-type jacket, the fronts elongated into

Chanel, on the stairs in rue Cambon

points, heavily emphasised with gold braid. A burgundy suede outfit with huge crushed velvet flowers at the neck – echoing Gabrielle's preference for artificial flowers, not bruised real petals. Simple swirling capes of the type she made at Deauville half a century ago, waistcoats covered in gold chains, fringed hems, short skirts, worn over matching thick tights. Gabrielle hated the mini, exposing the ugliest join in a woman's body, but Lagerfeld layered his skirts, and the short mid-thigh length was covered with floating pleats, split at the centre, reaching down to the feet, which would have placated her. After all, in the 1910s it was Gabrielle who put women into 'garçonne' dresses, shockingly, for the era, revealing the ankle. Then a suit with a gorgeous silk blouse, vast double bows at the neck and also at the front of the waist, homage to the Chanel look, but exaggerated, playing on our familiarity with the signatures. Long, long lines of pleated skirts, side-fastened with a tumbling line of gilt buttons. Complications of dresses with long pleats, covered with draped sections extending from the bodice, floating points wrapping round the bodice and the hips.

My favourite: a simple long shirt-waist style dress, constructed with flat pleats from the shoulder to the hem, fastened all down the centre front with big flat mother-of-pearl buttons. Gabrielle Chanel's legacy is being lovingly and brilliantly served by Karl Lagerfeld, unexpectedly in that he is a man (and Gabrielle tended to disapprove of male designers) and not even French: of German and Swedish ancestry.

After the collection, a visit to Gabrielle's apartment in the rue Cambon, kept exactly as she left it, a shrine. The door to her apartment stands at the head of the stairs, leading up from the showroom below. As one moves up the staircase, the panels of glass fracture and repeat the images, playfully, like the endless vistas of female beauty in a Busby Berkeley film, or like the distorted planes of a Cubist canvas. The door is mirrored on both sides, a reminder, once in the apartment, of the necessity of reflected images in the salon below. I found the interior less luxuriously intimidating than it is often pictured. Certainly, the luxury of the coromandel screens, mounted on the wall of her dining room, and cutting off the corners of her sitting room, impress the visitor. The gold-washed walls and beige suede sofa are as modern and stylish as when they were first chosen – Gabrielle was ahead of her time in her use of colours in her décor.

But Gabrielle's apartment is not a showplace. It has the atmosphere of an intimate, private place, a revealing reflection of her hidden spirituality. Religious objects cover the surfaces: a cross in gilt, a serene Buddha on top of shelves of leather bound books. There are objects of superstition too: a huge globe of crystal, mounted on the back of three silver lions: a head of a lion (Leo was her star sign) inside a mock gilt frame, a small brass lion reclining on the dining table. Typical of her, simple inexpensive objects jostle the valuable objets d'art on every surface: a little shepherd and his jewelled flock of sheep huddled on a tiny ground of lapis lazuli – a gift from a friend in her atelier. On another table gilt boxes for cigarettes marked with the arms of the Duke of Westminster, and elsewhere, tiny enamelled boxes, gold inside, a similar trick of taste as making a mink-lined mackintosh.

By the fireplace stands a sheaf of wheat; every year in her later life Gabrielle would visit the region of her birth, the Cévennes, and bring back the last sheaf of wheat gathered by the farmworkers. The apartment is full of images of nature's prolificacy, a pantheistic collection of animals: frogs, camels, monkeys, horses, a pair of life-size deer in varnished wood, baroque pearls set in a gilded cage, fashioned into love-birds.

The naked Greek marble torso of a woman dominates the sitting room. Bereft of arms and legs, it stands an essential, white body, small-bosomed, with athletic thighs, a boyish figure, like Gabrielle herself. It is placed between golden wheatsheafs, making the mantelpiece a mini-altar to fecundity, a celebration of womanhood in Gabrielle's own image.

A new crisis is being confronted in the Chanel empire. Copies of Gabrielle's work are now so widespread and form such a great industry, that the house is trying to protect the real creations, dedicatedly produced to her standards. A promising unprecedented lawsuit has given the house the right to protect Chanel designs even when they are unlabelled, not carrying any recognisable trademark like the twin 'Cs' linked back to back. It is the first time the French courts have recognised the need to protect the essential style – without the need for a label. No other couturier's work could ever stand the test of this degree of recognition, least of all, more than a decade after their death.

Yes, Gabrielle was pleased to be imitated, but in her day this was a question of compliment, woman to woman, on an individual scale. Besides, the real thing could only be purchased from her own salon, and the situation was controllable and limited. But in the 1960s, after her comeback, the English company of Wallis made a fortune out of cheaper copies of Chanel suits. There was no agreement between the house of Chanel and this company – Chanel was not happy with the plagiarism: it was not a homage to her, as the English press described it at the time. Just as Gabrielle was incensed by the Bourjois company making a huge profit from her name, so now the House of Chanel resists the enormous gains made internationally by others on the back of the name. 'Chanel' is in danger of becoming an adjective for a wide range of inferior, imitative products. However, the complexity of Lagerfeld's designs and the exquisite, exclusive fabrics he uses will always separate the real thing from the fake.

I watch the run through of a video interview Gabrielle Chanel gave to Jacques Chazot for French television in 1968. Naturally Gabrielle railed against the horrors of the mini-skirt, the general unkemptness of modern women, and the utter banality of the pop music explosion. Yet there were little revelations in her physical presence. She talks constantly, to mask her shyness. She folds a linen handkerchief precisely into a thin line, doubles it at the centre into a V, and carefully inserts it in the sleeve of her suit, so that two matched ends fall over her hand. A gesture of precision, a nervous ritual that fails to mask her desire for order and self-discipline.

On the way back to London, I read a moving portrait of Chanel by the French novelist Michel Déon, in *Bagages pour Vancouver*. One Christmas Eve, late in Gabrielle's life, he was dressing to go out to dinner with a girlfriend. Gabrielle telephoned him – a rare event, since it was her custom to let people make contact with her. She was alone. He was summoned to dine with her at the Hôtel Ritz. Such was her magnetism that he abandoned his plans and met her at the rue Cambon apartment – solitary, having let her staff go to their own festivities. Quite terrified by the realisation that she had turned down a multitude of invitations, and unexpectedly, had failed to secure the right company for this ritualistic evening. Dismayed at her predicament.

They walked back to the Ritz. The dining room was full. The maître d'hôtel was *désolé* but all he could offer Mademoiselle was a simple supper in her room. Gabrielle retired, leading Michel to her rooms, explaining with disapproval that, in her day, families fasted before midnight mass, and only ate together afterwards, in the small hours. It was a disgrace to see people stuffing themselves, oblivious of the significance of the eve of Christmas. So the couple supped their bowls of soup, broke a little bread, and became mildly intoxicated on Dom Perignon. The evening wore on: Michel Déon despaired of escaping to his female companion, his party of the night. He began to nod with the effect of the alcohol.

'Shame on you!' Gabrielle scolded suddenly. 'Haven't you any shame at your age? Go on, go and amuse yourself instead of hanging about with an old beast like me.' It was midnight when Michel Déon left her, the streets were cold, his girlfriend no doubt giving up hope had vanished, and he returned alone to his hotel, not in the least put out.

For Michel Déon, as for so many men before him, the attraction of Gabrielle Chanel was to be found in her enchantment. He believes that none of her biographers have done justice to her extraordinary magnetism, her magical, fairy-like quality, that literally held people captive. They planned to write a book together, in her last years, except that Gabrielle was certain that what the world, and particularly America, wanted, was nothing more than an exposé of her

fantasies. Michel Déon reminds us of 'her generosity, of such great delicacy, her remarkable intuition in music, in poetry, in theatre, and of course, in fashion'. Only painting barely interested her – though he too noted, as I did, one small canvas, negligently propped above a bookcase in her sitting room, unframed, a single ear of corn, painted by Salvador Dali. A classic, simple picture, 'not emerging from a runny Camembert. . . .'

But painting interests me. After my meeting at the salon, I walked to the Musée d'Orsay, and luckily advised by friends to take this extraordinarily celebratory Parisian gallery in a restrained first encounter, I climbed to the topmost gallery, and was overwhelmed by the beauty of the Impressionists' women. Not romanticised and inert, but active: ballerinas, barmaids, gardeners, mothers kissing babies, ingénues playing the piano – never passive, never boring. *She* had a terror of boredom, of being bored. Better to attack and cause sensation, than to let a day pass, undistinguished by no emotion. These images coalesced with those of Gabrielle's own making; she too wished to make women feminine, to celebrate their femininity, by ensuring that they were well-dressed, certainly to please

Coco Chanel in old age, photographed by Henri Cartier-Bresson

men, but not at the cost of their freedom. Chanel's women can hurry through the day, climb in and out of cars, work at their careers, meet friends they adore, and always present themselves with undiminished elegance and simplicity.

Having so recently experienced the extraordinary endurance of Gabrielle's personality, the devotion of the staff who live in the shadow of her memory, barely able to recall the physical presence of their mistress, I was glad that my parting image of Gabrielle Chanel was this: the still compelling charm of the woman, even a few years before her death, that kept a sensitive and devoted man friend willing to throw up all his plans just for the privilege of a simple Christmas night in her presence. I felt I could close my attempt at portraiture leaving her with that little shame she confessed, that she was too old to detain a charming man, and yet knowing, with a secret delight, that she had once again succeeded in her playful, poignant seduction.

BIBLIOGRAPHY

Baillen, Claude	*Chanel Solitaire* 1973
Ballard, Bettina	*In My Fashion* 1960
Boucher, F.	*History of Costume in the West* 1987
Boucourechliev, André	*Stravinsky* 1987
Buckle, Richard	*Diaghilev* 1979
Carter, Ernestine	*Magic Names of Fashion* 1980
Charles-Roux, Edmonde	*Chanel (L'Irregulière, 1974)*
Charles-Roux, Edmonde	*Chanel and her World* 1976
Colette	*Prisons et Paradis* 1935
Déon, Michel	*Bagages pour Vancouver* 1985
Field, Leslie	*Bendor, Duke of Westminster* 1983
Galante, Pierre	*Les Années Chanel* 1972
Garland, Madge	*The Indecisive Decade* 1968
Glynn, Prudence	*In Fashion* 1978
Haedrich, Marcel	*Coco Chanel* 1972
Kennett, Frances	*Secrets of the Couturiers* 1984
Kochno, Boris	*Diaghilev and the Ballets Russes* 1971
Lynam, Ruth	*Paris Fashion* 1972
McDowell, Colin	*Directory of 20th-Century Fashion* 1984
O'Hara, Georgina	*The Encyclopaedia of Fashion* 1986
Morand, Paul	*Venises* 1971
Poiret, Paul	*My First Fifty Years* 1931
Reverdy, Pierre	*En Vrac* 1956
Reverdy, Pierre	*Le Livre de Mon Bord* 1948
Sert, Misia	*Misia par Misia* 1953
Woolman Chase, Edna	*Always in Vogue* 1954

INDEX